The Midwest Gardener's

Book of Lists

The Midwest Gardener's

BOOK OF LISTS

Susan McClure

Taylor Publishing Company
Dallas, Texas

*To midwesterners who love this dramatic part of the country
and enjoy making the most of it in
their yards and gardens.*

Library of Congress Cataloging-in-Publication Data

    McClure, Susan, 1957–
        The midwest gardener's book of lists / Susan McClure.
          p.   cm.
        Includes index.
        ISBN 0-87833-985-X
        1. Landscape plants—Middle West. 2. Landscape gardening—Middle West. I. Title
    SB408.M34 1998
    635'.0977—dc21   97-47321
                                                        CIP

Designed by David Timmons

Printed in the United States of America
10 9 8 7 6 5 4 3 2 1

CONTENTS

ACKNOWLEDGMENTS

To Hardy Eshbaugh and my other botany professors at Miami University and my grandfather who was the great gardener in my family, to experiences from gardens grown in Oxford and Cleveland, Ohio, and now in Indiana, and outstanding public gardens like Cleveland Botanical Garden, Stan Hywet Hall, Gardenview Horticultural Park, Chicago Botanic Garden, Holden Arboretum, Morton Arboretum, and others too numerous to name, I am grateful for a rich education and Midwestern perspective on gardening. Thanks also to Lake County Nursery Exchange, wholesalers in Perry, Ohio, who detailed plant lists provided much inspiration. And to all the other nurserymen, designers, and enthusiasts who offered advice and lists—I am deeply grateful!

The Midwest Gardener's

Book of Lists

INTRODUCTION

Creating a new landscape or updating an old one can be a little like starting to write a book. There are so many things to consider that you can become overwhelmed and avoid beginning at all. The secret to overcoming starting line frustration is the list—civilized mankind's greatest organizational tool. Once you see your planting options, itemized on a piece of paper or a computer screen, you have a place to begin. You can check books and catalogs to find out more about the plants you have listed. You can imagine different listed plants in your garden or sketch them into your landscape plan to see how they would fit. You can cross out those that aren't appropriate and focus on choosing wisely from the ones that remain. Whether you are looking for one specimen shrub, a dozen border perennials, or a hundred bedding plants, the lists in *The Midwest Gardener's Book of Lists* will get you going.

You'll find lists of annuals, perennials, ferns, herbs and ornamental vegetables, bulbs, ground covers, vines, roses, shrubs, and trees, all specifically selected to be well suited for the Midwest. If your house is surrounded by large trees, check those lists of plants that thrive in shade. Stuck about what to do with hard clay? Look for tips to help you modify clay and lists of plants that will thrive in it. Are deer turning your yard into a snackbar? You'll find lists of plants they are less likely to snack on.

Other lists help you find the right plant for a particular landscape use, by selecting them by form or color, for instance. Still other lists help you plan a succession of flowers, fruit, and fall color for magnificence through the seasons. You'll also find lists and tips from over fifty Midwestern gardening experts, sharing information about which plants have thrived for them, new and uncommon plants to look for, and new perspectives on Midwestern gardening.

Plants included in this book run the gamut from readily available plants found in almost any garden center to specialized plants—new, old, or rare—that may need to be sought out through specialty nurseries. Your local landscaper or all-purpose nursery can help you find the common plants; unusual plants may have to be ordered through mail order catalogs or from nurseries that specialize in certain hard-to-find species.

THE MIDWESTERN CLIMATE

How many times have you picked up a great gardening book, pored over its pages, and absorbed its information only to find out that it was written in England for a vastly different climate? Midwestern weather has a personality all its own—cold winters and hot summers—and a special array of plants that grow well in it. Getting in tune with your climate—learning its highs and lows and its wet and dry spells—helps make you a successful gardener. Understanding your local weather patterns teaches you to choose plants that will thrive in the climate and conditions that are right outside your door—not in New England, Philadelphia, or Texas. That is what this book is all about!

The Midwest includes a range of climatic zones with their own individual peculiarities. For me it's paradise to drive down to flower-filled southern Indiana in late April when my yard in northern Indiana is still sulky and cold. Minnesota is even colder than my hometown, and gardeners there usually find summer arriving later and leaving earlier than those in more southerly zones.

The simplest way to find plants that will do well in your particular climate is to see where you fall on the United States Department of Agriculture Climatic Zone Map, which is based on the average winter low temperatures for different regions of the country. Skirting the southern portion of the Midwest and including southern Ohio, Indiana, Missouri, and Illinois is Zone 6, with winter lows of -10 degrees F. Zone 5, which sweeps across the middle of the region and includes northern Ohio, Indiana, Illinois, Missouri, southern Iowa, and much of Michigan, has winter lows of -10 to -20 degrees F. The upper Midwest, including northern Iowa and much of Wisconsin and Minnesota, can have temperatures as low as -30 degrees F.

Because of these gradual but important differences, plants hardy in the lower Midwest may not thrive in the upper Midwest. If you live in the northern zones, double check plant hardiness with a local nurseryman or Cooperative Extension agent before you set out to buy any plants.

Small areas of climatic variation, called *microclimates*, explain why peach orchards and vineyards thrive in western Michigan, northern Indiana along Lake Michigan, and along the southern shoreline of Lake Erie but not farther inland. These are areas of microclimate with milder winters and longer, frost-free autumns, protected by the proximity to the Great Lakes.

Microclimates can cover large areas or be contained in a single town, a hilltop or valley, or even a backyard. Western Chicago is solidly within Zone 5 while the Chicago Gold Coast (also called the Chicago banana belt) near Lake Michigan is more like Zone 6. Other microclimates occupy smaller areas. City temperatures tend to stay warmer than outlying areas, allowing city gardeners to get a head start on country gardeners by planting their impatiens a week or two earlier. A garden on the sunny, south side of your house is likely to be warmer in winter than one in the middle of the yard. A garden on the shady, north side of a building or wall will warm up more slowly in spring and stay cooler in summer.

SOIL SPECIFICATIONS

Finding plants that will thrive depends on more than just hardiness. Thoroughly hardy plants, like some chrysanthemums and asters, will fail if planted in heavy and soggy clay soil. Identifying the type of soil in your garden and finding plants well suited to it is another factor that separates green thumbers from would-be gardeners.

The easiest and best way to understand your soil is with a test, which reveals the structure,

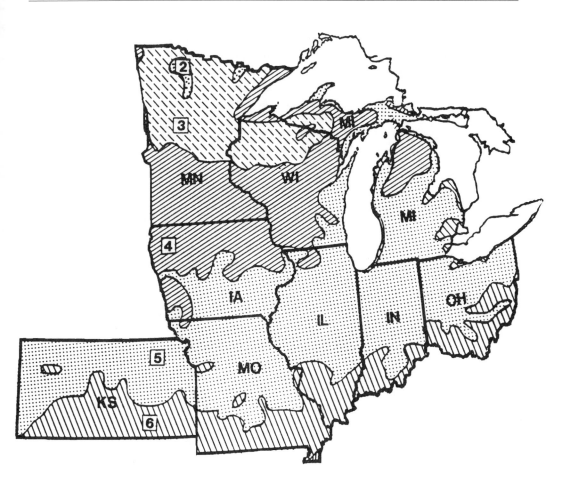

RANGE OF AVERAGE ANNUAL MINIMUM
TEMPERATURES FOR EACH ZONE

ZONE 1	BELOW −50°F		
ZONE 2	−50°	TO	−40°
ZONE 3	−40°	TO	−30°
ZONE 4	−30°	TO	−20°
ZONE 5	−20°	TO	−10°
ZONE 6	−10°	TO	0°
ZONE 7	0°	TO	10°
ZONE 8	10°	TO	20°
ZONE 9	20°	TO	30°
ZONE 10	30°	TO	40°
ZONE 11	ABOVE 40°		

acidity, and nutrient levels of the soil. For little extra cost, you can also find out how much organic matter is in your soil—5 percent being the minimum needed for good growing conditions. To learn more about soil testing, check with your Cooperative Extension Service, usually listed under federal or county offices in the phone book yellow pages.

You can get a general idea of your soil type by studying its characteristics as you work with it. Clay soil has a slippery feel when wet and is heavy, dense, and slow to dry out in spring. It can be made lighter and fluffier with the addition of plenty of organic material such as compost, peat moss, and leaf mold. Sandy soils—light, loose, and often low in nutrients—warm up earlier in spring but dry out quickly. Sandy soil can be amended with organic matter to make them richer and moister.

Sun and Shade

Plants draw their energy from the sun so making sure they get enough light is of vital importance. Plants that need full sun must have at least six hours of sun a day. Where there is less sunlight available, shop for plants that do well in shade or light shade. After a year or two, a sun-loving rose pushed into a dark corner is unlikely to look as good as a shade-loving oak leaf hydrangea.

New and Old Names

In most of these lists, with the exception of certain ornamental edibles and cultivars, you'll find Latin botanical names beside common names. Using Latin names when you shop for plants makes you look like you know what you're doing, but their importance goes even deeper. Latin botanical names provide a universal method of communication, as clear and effective in Mexico and England as in America. Common names may vary by region, neighborhood, and household and one plant can easily be mistaken for another. For example, hardy ageratums (*Eupatorium coelestinum*) are not ageratums at all but a relative of Joe-Pye weed (*Eupatorium maculatum*), and are easily identified as such by looking at their botanical name.

Another problem with common names is they can be too general to allow you to order a specific species or cultivar, such as the wonderful dwarf Shasta daisy, 'Little Silver Princess'. Botanical names allow you to specify exactly what you want. If you go to a nursery and asked for sage, you could end up with gray-leaved culinary sage, a pineapple-scented herb, a blue- or red-flowered annual, a violet-flowered perennial, or one of dozens of less common types of sage. Using Latin botanical and cultivar names ensures that you will get exactly what you want.

There are, however, occasional complications with botanical names. These complications arise among plant taxonomists and botanists devoted to studying plant species and botanical relationships. Sometimes new findings occasion name changes to reflect these discoveries. These new names reach some of the more progressive nurseries and books almost immediately, while many other nurseries and plantsmen staunchly cling to the original names that gardeners find more familiar. One of the most unsettling changes of recent years concerns the florists chrysanthemum (*Chrysanthemum hortorum*) now properly called *Dendranthema* x *grandiflorum*. Shasta daisies (*Chrysanthemum* x *superba*) have been changed to *Leucanthemum* x *superba*.

This book uses classic botanical names listed in *Hortus III* (1986 edition), a 1300-page naming bible considered the ultimate reference by many horticulturists and gardeners. There are occasional updates from the more recent *Royal Horticultural Society Index of Garden Plants* (1995 edition).

BOOKS AND REFERENCE RESOURCES

Supplement your garden lists with solid advice and plant information. With books like the following, gardening experts will always be at your beck and call.

MUST HAVE FOR BASIC REFERENCE

I am quick to refer to the following books for gardening reference. Although written for a national audience, they have solid information for the Midwestern gardener.

The Herb Gardener: A Guide for All Seasons, Susan McClure, Storey Communications, Pownal, Vermont, 1996. OK, I wrote it but it is one of the best complete growing guides for dozens of useful herbs.

Manual of Woody Landscape Plants, Michael Dirr, Stipes Publishing, Champaign, Illinois, 1990. Dr. Dirr, now a resident of Georgia, spent many years in Illinois and offers advice suited to our region. This encyclopedic book remains a classic—thorough and well founded.

Rodale's Illustrated Encyclopedia of Perennials, Ellen Phillips and C. Colston Burrell, Rodale Press, Emmaus, Pennsylvania, 1993. Burrell, a Minnesota resident, adds a decidedly Midwestern slant on this complete and nicely illustrated guide to growing perennials.

FOR INSPIRATION

Photographs and descriptions of stunning Midwestern gardens prove what can be done with the Midwestern soil and climate. For the inspiration and ideas that these books can provide, I recommend the following.

Gardens of the Heartland, Laura Martin, Abbeville Press, New York, 1996. Thirty public gardens are captured in prose and fantastic photography.

Midwest Gardens, Pamela Wolfe, Chicago Review Press, Chicago, Illinois, 1991. Twenty-two private gardens are explored by this well-known Midwestern author and teacher.

FOR INSTRUCTION

These are books that provide basic gardening information and advice from Midwestern writers and horticulturists.

WITHIN THE REGION

Denny McKeown's Complete Guide to Midwest Gardening, Denny McKeown, Taylor Publishing, Dallas, Texas, 1985. McKeown, nurseryman and radio personality, offers a colorful and complete guide to Midwest gardening and landscaping.

Gardening in the Lower Midwest: A Practical Guide for the New Zones 5 and 6, Diane Heilenman, Indiana University Press, Bloomington and Indianapolis, Indiana, 1994. Heilenman, a garden writer for the *Louisville Courier Journal* in Kentucky, covers plants, techniques, and gardens for the warmer end of the Midwest.

Gardening: Plains and Upper Midwest, Roger Vick, Fulcrum Publishing, Golden, Colorado, 1991. On the other end of the scale are northern climates with blazingly hot summers and bitterly cold winters. This book draws on the author's hands-on experience to address making the garden grow.

Growing Trees on the Great Plains, Margaret Brazell, Fulcrum Publishing, Golden, Colorado, 1992. Where the climate is cold and dry, you'll be able to use Brazell's growing tips and plant recommendations to overcome obstacles.

Marlyn's Garden: Seasoned Advice for Achieving Spectacular Results in the Midwest, Marlyn

Dicken Sachtjen, Chicago Review Press, Chicago Illinois, 1994. This personality-rich book covers the gardening spectrum—soil, shrubs, prairies, perennials, and edibles—through the lessons learned by a lifelong Wisconsin gardener.

Plants of the Chicago Region, Floyd Swink and Gerould Wilhelm, Indiana Academy of Science, Indianapolis, Indiana, 1994. This thick tome provides identification and information for thousands of plants of the greater Chicago region, including northwest Indiana, southwest Michigan, and southeast Wisconsin. In this rich area where eastern deciduous forest meets western prairie and northern forests, each region has its own special plant life.

Possum in the Pawpaw Tree, B. Rosie Lerner and Beverly Netzhammer, Purdue University Press, 1994. Lerner, a Purdue University Cooperative Extension Service horticulture specialist, and Netzhammer, a landscape designer and master gardener, have compiled useful hints and answers to common questions in this friendly month-by-month gardening guide.

MAGAZINES

Many larger Midwestern cities are likely to have a local magazine or newsletter of special interest to gardeners. Botanical gardens, arboreta, and plant societies send members informative and timely hints in their publications. There also are independent magazines and newsletters, including the following two excellent choices for the Chicago area.

Chicagoland Gardening, PO Box 208, Downers Grove, IL 60515-0208: Written for northern Indiana, Illinois, and southern Wisconsin, this handsome magazine covers all aspects of gardening—how-to and theory—with fresh ideas on landscaping. It highlights some of the best gardens in the area and often has delightful recipes for garden-fresh produce.

The Garden Letter: Green Thoughts for the Northern Gardener, One Crow's Hill, St. Paul, MN 55102: This award-winning magazine offers a potpourri of short articles, tips, recipes, history, travel, and great advice. Published four times a year.

The Weedpatch Gazette, PO Box 339, Richmond, IL 60071-0339: Each issue is devoted to a different topic—oaks, historic landscapes, unusual annuals, and more. Articles are written by horticultural experts, many from the Chicago area, and include lists of plants and sources.

Specialty subjects

When you need to get up close and familiar with a particular group of plants, these are good reference works.

Best Flowers for Midwest Gardens, Laara Duggan, Chicago Review Press, Chicago, Illinois, 1996. Compiled from years of gardening journals, these are flowers and techniques that will stand up to Midwestern weather.

Flowering Trees for the Midwest, Mary Walker and F.A. Giles, University of Illinois Special Publication 68, Urbana-Champaign, Illinois, 1985. Although somewhat dated, many of the trees mentioned remain classics.

Gardener's Guide, Midwest, Louise Carter and Joanne Lawson, Fulcrum Publishing, Golden, Colorado, annual gardening calendars. Beautiful photographs and timely tips help coordinate your schedule and encourage your green thumb.

Ground Covers for the Midwest, T.B. Voigt, Betty Hamilton, and F.A. Giles, University of Illinois Special Publication 65, Urbana-Champaign, Illinois, 1983. An encyclopedia of ground covers ideal for the Midwest.

Large Flowering Shrubs for the Midwest, Sharon Irwin Morrisey and F.A. Giles, University of Illinois Special Publication 74, Urbana-Champaign, Illinois. This encyclopedia of shrubs is ideal for the Midwest.

INTERNET RESOURCES

An ever-expanding variety of online resources await your inspection on the Internet—nursery catalogs, magazine articles, gardening encyclopedias, and even research reports. Accessing this information takes time and a good web browser.

For general information on gardening, you can go straight to special addresses such as those for the big Missouri Botanical Garden site or for the latest reports from Midwestern Cooperative Extension Service offices like those run by Ohio State University and Michigan State University. You can also search for information on a particular subject. Don't be surprised if you end up with more material than you want. A general search on *scilla* (a spring bulb), for example, came up with about 50,000 references, most of them too obscure to be of any real use. For a faster and more focused search, plus a variety of other interesting stuff, check out special garden sites like Time Inc., Virtual Garden, or GardenNet. They include gardening articles of timely interest, places for gardeners to chat or have questions answered, and databases of gardening information. You also can use the Internet to find gardening-related excerpts from Midwestern publications like the *Detroit News* and advice from organizations like the American Rose Society.

MATCHING PLANTS TO ARCHITECTURE

WITH JANET SMEDLEY

Throughout this book you'll find lists of plants organized according to their formal or informal shapes, bright or muted colors, historical significance, or purely contemporary attraction. With a careful eye for form and overall impression, you can coordinate the effects of your plantings to enhance your home's architecture and create an attractive, all-encompassing harmony.

Architect Janet Smedley of St. John, Indiana, enjoys matching plants to different types of architecture. She agrees with British gardener Penelope Hobhouse, who said that a successful garden should have an enlightened overall vision so that the plants and layout become inseparable. When the architecture of the house is sympathetic to the garden, the entire property will be in harmony. Smedley has developed the following plant lists to coordinate with different types of architecture.

 "Look at your house and start there. Consider the historical style and spirit. Then use those design attitudes to draw a garden design into your landscape."
Janet Smedley, architect and landscape designer from St. John, Indiana

Formal Architecture

Formal homes usually have balanced symmetrical facades and classical details such as pedimented doors and windows, pilasters, and colonnaded porches. A formal garden design, like those of the grand palatial gardens of Europe, works best with this type of architecture. There is a visible order to the beds and walkways, and evergreens are often used to anchor garden features and maintain year-round interest. A formal layout usually features axial lines, which radiate from the house, and views that are revealed in sequence as you walk through the garden and stop at a focal point like a bench, fountain, or arbor. The garden may be connected to the house with paving.

Pure geometric forms such as circles, rectangles, and squares all contribute to a formal ambiance, as do a repetition of forms and patterns. Additional interest can be added in the form of vistas; parterres; walks with focal points; brick paving; terracing for changes in level; and an overall purity of color in your choice of flowering and foliage plants.

SHRUBS

Hollies (*Ilex* spp.)
Dwarf globe arborvitae (*Thuja occidentalis* 'Pygmy Globe' and others)

ROSES

New Dawn climbing rose (*Rosa* 'New Dawn')
Othello (Austin) rose (*Rosa* × 'Othello')
Madam Plantier rose (*Rosa alba* 'Madam Plantier')
Bourbon rose (*Rosa* × *borboniana* 'Variegata de Bologna')

PERENNIALS

Globe
Arborvitae

Lady's mantle (*Alchemilla mollis*)
Pinks (*Dianthus* spp.)
Gaura (*Gaura Lindheimeri*)
Mount Everest lily (*Lilium* 'Mount Everest')
Catchfly (*Lychnis* spp.)
Obedience plant (*Physostegia virginiana* 'Alba')
Veronica (*Veronica* spp.)

HERBS

Silver Brocade artemisia (*Artemisia* 'Silver Brocade')
Lavender (*Lavandula* spp.)
Santolina (*Santolina* spp.)
Lamb's ears (*Stachys byzantina*)
Creeping thyme (*Thymus* spp.)

VINES AND GROUND COVERS

English ivy (*Hedera helix*)
Climbing hydrangea (*Hydrangea petiolaris*)

Romantic Architecture

Romantic architecture encompasses those grand Victorian style houses with their asymmetrical facades, steeply pitched roofs, gables, and textured wall surfaces. To complement a romantic style home, private, secluded gardens that exclude the outside world are ideal. Romantic gardens feature a sense of mystery that is created by a layout that never allows the whole garden to be visible at a glance. Use curving walks with forking paths and hidden views to excite the imagination; fill the garden with soft colors, shade, and antique or distressed materials. Allow paths to follow the natural contours of the land and include ponds and architectural follies to add interest. Appeal to the senses with the sound of water, fragrant flowers, and an abundance of densely planted flowers.

SHRUBS

Lilac (*Syringa* spp.)
Korean spice viburnum (*Viburnum Carlesii*)

ROSES

Abraham Darby (Austin) rose (*Rosa* × 'Abraham Darby')
Constance Spry (Austin) rose (*Rosa* × 'Constance Spry')
Graham Thomas (Austin) rose (*Rosa* × 'Graham Thomas')
Kiftsgate climbing rose (*Rosa* 'Kiftsgate')
Damask rose (*Rosa damascena* 'Madame Hardy')
Red leaf rose (*Rosa glauca*)

PERENNIALS

Columbine (*Aquilegia* spp.)
Delphinium (*Delphinium grandiflorum*)
White old fashioned bleeding heart (*Dicentra spectabilis* 'Alba')
Johnson's Blue hardy geranium (*Geranium* × 'Johnson's Blue')
Siberian iris (*Iris sibirica*)
Catmint (*Nepeta* × *Faassenii*; *N.* × *Mussinii*)
Oriental poppy (*Papaver orientale*)
Russian sage (*Perovskia atriplicifolia*)
Phlox (*Phlox* spp.)
Scabiosa (*Scabiosa* spp.)
Violets (*Viola* spp.)

HERBS

Artemisia (*Artemisia* spp.)
English lavender (*Lavandula angustifolia*)
Santolina (*Santolina* spp.)
Lamb's ears (*Stachys byzantina*)

VINES

Comtesse de Bouchard clematis (*Clematis* 'Comtesse de Bouchard')
Sweet autumn clematis (*Clematis maximowicziana* syn. *paniculata*)
Perle d'Azur clematis (*Clematis* 'Perle d'Azur')
Trumpet honeysuckle (*Lonicera sempervirens*)

Cottage Style

Cottage style homes include farm houses, Tudor houses, ranches, and bungalows. Reflecting the rural past, cottage gardens should be filled with sunshine, flowers, fruit, herbs, and vegetables all blended together to form a profusion of color and form. Planting and pruning should give the appearance of a simplistic, natural, haphazard effect. Keep paving materials informal: random stepping stones or loose fill materials like gravel or wood chips are best.

An easy relationship between the house and neighborhood can be made with a low fence, an open gate, and an inviting bench, making the garden a place for lingering amid the roses.

SHRUBS

Butterfly bush (*Buddleia Davidii*)

ROSES

Paul Neyron rose (*Rosa* 'Paul Neyron')
Mary Rose (Austin) rose (*Rosa* × 'Mary Rose')
Heritage (Austin) rose (*Rosa* × 'Heritage')
Cecil Brunner climbing rose (*Rosa* 'Cecil Brunner')
Theresa Bugnet rugosa rose (*Rosa rugosa* 'Theresa Bugnet')

PERENNIALS

Alma Potschke aster (*Aster* 'Alma Potschke')
Foxglove (*Digitalis purpurea*)
Purple coneflower (*Echinacea purpurea*)
Wargrave Pink hardy geranium (*Geranium* 'Wargrave Pink')
Blazing star (*Liatris* spp.)
Bee balm (*Monarda didyma*)
Balloon flower (*Platycodon grandiflorus*)

HERBS

Garlic chives (*Allium tuberosum*)
English lavender (*Lavandula Angustifolia*)
Berggarten sage (*Salvia officinalis* 'Berggarten')
Santolina (*Santolina* spp.)
Thyme (*Thymus* spp.)

EDIBLES

Onions/Leeks (*Allium* spp.)
Strawberries (*Fragaria* × *ananassa*)
Sunflowers (*Helianthus annuus*)

Sunflower

Lettuce (*Lactuca sativa*)
Tomatoes (*Lycopersicon esculentum*)
Parsley (*Petroselinium crispum*)
Raspberries/Blackberries (*Rubus* spp.)
Pansy (*Viola* × *Wittrockiana*)

Contemporary Style

Contemporary style homes include any whose architecture speaks boldly of aesthetics and design over pure utility; this style may include beach houses, geometrically design modern homes, and mission style houses.

The contemporary design garden sweeps up to the house, joins with it, and links it inextricably to its environment, using native plants and interesting combinations of color, foliage, and texture to complement the building style. Inspiration comes from the site itself—a big old oak tree or wetland, for instance. The space is designed to connect interior and exterior, encouraging one to look outward where the drift and flow of natural plant material, vivid colors, expansive views, and rugged textures link the indoors to outdoor living areas such as decks and patios.

ROSES

The Fairy rose (*Rosa polyantha* 'The Fairy')
Alba rugosa rose (*Rosa rugosa* 'Alba')
Fru Dagmar Hastrup rugosa rose (*Rosa rugosa* 'Fru Dagmar Hastrup')

PERENNIALS

NOTE: Native plants are always appropriate for this kind of landscape. See the list of Neil Duboll's Suggested Native Prairie Plants in the Perennials and Ornamental Grasses chapter.

Yarrow

Yarrow (*Achillea* spp.)
Artemisia (*Artemisia* spp.)
Astilbe (*Astilbe* spp.)
Chrysanthemums (*Chrysanthemum* spp.; *Dendranthema* spp.)
Early Sunrise coreopsis (*Coreopsis grandiflora* 'Early Sunrise')
Purple coneflower (*Echinacea purpurea*)
Globe thistle (*Echinops Ritro*)
Sea holly (*Eryngium* spp.)
Oxeye daisy (*Heliopsis helianthoides*)
Daylilies (*Hemerocallis* spp.)
Iris (*Iris* spp.)
Maiden grass (*Miscanthus* spp.)
Poppies (*Papaver* spp.)
Golden coneflowers (*Rudbeckia* spp.)
Sage (*Salvia* spp.)

ANNUALS

Cosmos (*Cosmos* spp.)
Sunflowers (*Helianthus* spp.)

VINES

American bittersweet (*Celastrus scandens*)
Honeysuckle (*Lonicera* spp.)
Sweet autumn clematis (*Clematis maximowicziana* syn. *paniculata*)
Perle d'Azur clematis (*Clematis* 'Perle d'Azur')

TREES

Trees, the plant world's counterpart to the mythical Paul Bunyon sans the giant blue ox, are big, bold, and magnificent. When planted where they will thrive, trees become permanent fixtures, often lasting longer than even the houses they are planted next to. A lifespan of a century or more is not uncommon for oaks and hickories, which can be dated by counting annual growth rings in the cross-sectioned trunks on display in any Midwestern nature center.

Having moved recently to a new neighborhood with stark acres of open grass, I miss large trees dearly; I miss their shade and the way they frame a house, making any home more attractive and more inviting. During the long, dull winter, I especially miss evergreens and the handsome branching patterns naked deciduous trees cast as shadows on the ground when the sun occasionally emerges.

Trees are more than shademakers; they can also be used as privacy screens, windbreaks, specimen plants, and as sources of fruit for both man and wildlife. Evergreens planted side by side can form a tall wall of foliage, providing more privacy than a fence and doing so less obtrusively. Spring flowering trees like crabapples and magnolias have handsome flowers that are most welcome after a long winter, and their moderate size makes them suitable for any yard. Trees can be chosen for their exceptional foliage, autumn color, spring or summer flowers, attractive berries and other handsome fruits, or for their outstanding bark—all characteristics worth considering.

When choosing a new tree, you can make sure that the time and money you invest is well spent by following a few simple rules.

• Make sure the tree is thoroughly hardy in your climate. Because trees grow for decades, sooner or later they will be exposed to the highest and lowest temperatures possible in your area and they must be able to survive unscathed.

• Freedom from pests and diseases is another priority. Choose trees that are known to be reliably pest and disease resistant.

• Plant trees in the site and soil they prefer. Adequate amounts of sunlight, soil moisture, and nutrients are essential for good growth and vigor. If stressed and growing poorly, even ordinarily trouble-free trees may succumb to problems.

• Trees with strong wood and widely angled branches are able to endure ice and wind storms without breaking apart. For safety's sake, don't plant trees too close to houses, other buildings, and utility lines so that an occasional toppling limb won't cause damage.

• Check with local nurserymen, Cooperative Extension Service agents, botanical gardens, or arboreta to find out how a particular prospect grows your area.

• Avoid trees with irritating or messy habits, such as those that shed large quantities of seeds, fruits, spent blossoms, or autumn leaves on rooftops, sidewalks, and driveways, or those that have sprawling surface roots that can heave up pavement. Either don't plant these varieties or site them where they won't cause problems.

Right Plant, Right Place

If your property is blessed with loose, loamy soil and a sunny location, you can choose from a great many trees. But where shade creeps in, the soil is poor, or the city looms large around your yard, you must look for trees best able to grow well under less than ideal circumstances. This section also includes trees that have irritating habits, such as surface roots and falling fruits, which are best known about in advance.

TREES THAT TOLERATE SHADE

Redbud

Where shadows limit sunshine, shade-tolerant or shade-loving trees thrive. A small tree rising gracefully at the edge of a shady grove and leaning slightly out toward the sun makes a lovely picture. Except for the Japanese black pine, these trees naturally grow in the dappled shade of woodlands, but many will do well in full sun.

Hedge maple (*Acer campestre*)
Serviceberry (*Amelanchier* spp.)
American hornbeam (*Carpinus caroliniana*)
Redbud (*Cercis canadensis*)
Fringe tree (*Chionanthus virginicus*)
Flowering dogwood (*Cornus florida*)
Sweet bay magnolia (*Magnolia virginiana*)
Japanese black pine (*Pinus Thunbergiana*)
Canadian hemlock (*Tsuga canadensis*)

NEIL NELSON'S TREES THAT CAST DAPPLED SHADE

Trees with sparse branching or small leaves that allow the sun to shine through and support the growth of wildflowers, ferns, hostas, or impatiens around their bases. These light-hearted options come from Neil Nelson, president of Insti-Trees Nurseries of Rhinelander, Wisconsin, which is devoted to developing and marketing genetically improved trees.

Gray birch (*Betula populifolia*)
Honey locust (*Gleditsia triacanthos*)
European larch (*Larix decidua*)
Tamarack (*Larix laricina*)

TREES FOR DRY SITES

Although the Midwest is not known for dry weather, there usually comes at least one stretch of midsummer drought every year. If dry spells are lengthy or repeated year after year, trees may be weakened by lack of moisture. In Cleveland, during 1996, many maples and ashes failed from droughts experienced several years earlier. Moisture deficiency is more problematic in sandy or gravel-rich soils and on well-drained slopes that retain little moisture. The solution is to plant deep-rooted or drought-tolerant trees.

Even these rugged survivors need a little pampering until well established. For at least a year after planting, mulch and eliminate the grass beneath the boughs to reduce water loss. Soak the planting site deeply during dry weather to encourage the roots to dig deep.

Hedge maple (*Acer campestre*)
Sweet birch (*Betula lenta*)
Hackberry (*Celtis occidentalis*)
Turkish filbert (*Corylus colurna*)
Smoke tree (*Cotinus Coggygria*)
Hawthorn (*Crataegus* spp.)
Russian olive (*Elaeagnus angustifolia*)
Hardy rubber tree (*Eucommia ulmoides*)
Green ash (*Fraxinus pennsylvanica*)
Thornless honey locust (*Gleditsia triacanthos* var. *inermis*)
Kentucky coffee tree (*Gymnocladus dioica*)
Goldenrain tree (*Koelreuteria paniculata*)
Eastern white pine (*Pinus strobus*)
Lacebark elm (*Ulmus parvifolia*)

A TREE WITH TOXIC ROOTS

Black walnut (*Juglans nigra*), valued for its lovely, hard wood, releases a phytotoxic compound called *juglone*, which kills tomatoes, alfalfa, and a number of other species that grow anywhere in the proximity of its wide-spreading roots. Fortunately, it doesn't bother Kentucky bluegrass, so black walnuts grow nicely in most lawns.

TREES WITH MANY SURFACE ROOTS

Some of the most troublesome trees are those with prominent roots that protrude above the surface of the soil. These exposed roots get scalped by the lawn mower (a jarring experience), can lift pavement, and can also honeycomb the upper layers of the soil, leaving little soil space for the roots of flowers, bulbs, or ground covers. Plant these trees well away from flower beds and paved areas.

Maples (*Acer* spp.)
American beech (*Fagus grandifolia*)
Sycamore (*Platanus occidentalis*)
Cottonwood (*Populus deltoides*)
Pin oak (*Quercus palustris*)
Bald cypress (*Taxodium distichum*)

American
Beech

TREES FOR MOIST SITES

Poorly drained clay, low areas, naturally boggy ground, and the banks of ponds and streams can be overly soggy for at least part of the year. A unique wetland, accessible via a boardwalk at Maumee Bay State Park, near Toledo, Ohio, has a hardwood forest that survives even though the roots are under six inches of water for most of the spring. These wet sites call for trees that can take a soaking and keep on growing. Bald cypress and willows will withstand continually wet soils, while hackberry is adaptable enough for wet or dry sites. Because most are heavy water users, irrigation when the ground dries up may be necessary for top performance.

Red maple (*Acer rubrum*)
Sugar maple (*Acer saccharum*)
Downy serviceberry (*Amelanchier arborea*)
River birch (*Betula nigra*)
American hornbeam (*Carpinus caroliniana*)
Hackberry (*Celtis occidentalis*)
Atlantic white cedar (*Chamaecyparis thyoides*)
Green ash (*Fraxinus pennsylvanica*)
Thornless honey locust (*Gleditsia triacanthos* var. *inermis*)
Kentucky coffee tree (*Gymnocladus dioica*)
American sweet gum (*Liquidambar Styraciflua*)
Sweet bay magnolia (*Magnolia virginiana*)
London plane tree (*Platanus* × *acerifolia*)
Sycamore (*Platanus occidentalis*)
Swamp white oak (*Quercus bicolor*)
Pin oak (*Quercus palustris*)
Willows (*Salix* spp.)
Bald cypress (*Taxodium distichum*)

Red Maple

TREES FOR HEAVY SOILS

Dense clay, common throughout the Midwest, can be soggy and poorly drained in wet weather and hard as a brick in dry weather. When building flower or shrub beds in clay, amendments are necessary to gentle its nature. But large trees will root well beyond any attempts at soil renovation. It's best just to accept what nature has wrought and start out with trees well suited to clay.

Hedge maple (*Acer campestre*)
Red maple (*Acer rubrum*)
River birch (*Betula nigra*)
Redbuds (*Cercis* spp.)
Hawthorn (*Crataegus* spp.)
American hornbeam (*Carpinus caroliniana*)
Russian olive (*Elaeagnus angustifolia*)
Hardy rubber tree (*Eucommia ulmoides*)
Green ash (*Fraxinus pennsylvanica*)

Thornless honey locust (*Gleditsia triacanthos* var. *inermis*)
Goldenrain tree (*Koelreuteria paniculata*)
Sweet gum (*Liquidambar Styraciflua*)
Spruce (*Picea* spp.)
London plane tree (*Platanus* × *acerifolia*)
Willows (*Salix* spp.)
Bald cypress (*Taxodium distichum*)

JUDY DEPUE'S TOP TEN TREES FOR NORTHERN INDIANA

In USDA Zone 5, winter temperatures occasionally drop to -20 F while in summer the mercury occasionally soars to 100 degrees F. There is more than a moderate amount of wind and ice and unreliable spurts of drought and monsoons that make growing conditions variable, at best. Under these less than ideal circumstances, certain trees exhibit exceptional performance. Here are ten tried-and-true favorites of Judy DePue, APLD Certified Professional Landscape Designer and owner of New Vistas Landscaping in Goshen, Indiana.

Flowering Dogwood

Red maple (*Acer rubrum* 'Red Sunset')
Downy Serviceberry (*Amelanchier arborea*)
River birch (*Betula nigra*)
Flowering dogwood (*Cornus florida* 'Cherokee' varieties)
Hawthorn (*Crataegus viridis* 'Winter King')
Star magnolia (*Magnolia stellata* 'Royal Star')
Crabapples (recommended for disease resistance and small fruits) (*Malus* spp. 'Prairiefire', 'Red Jewel', 'Centurion', 'Pink Princess', and 'Sugar Tyme')
Flowering pears (*Pyrus calleryana* 'Aristocrat' and 'Cleveland Select')
Fernleaf buckthorn (*Rhamnus Frangula* 'Asplenifolia')
Littleleaf linden (*Tilia cordata*)

"I operate with the belief that as trees, flowers, and shrubs come into bloom and the leaves turn beautiful colors, the people whose life paths take them nearby capture a moment of the refreshing beauty of nature to take with them as they face the tensions of their day."

Judy DePue, APLD Certified Garden Designer in northern Indiana

TREES WITH INCONVENIENT LITTER

Trees that drop twigs, fruit, seed pods, or large leaves may not create a stir in the woods, but if looming over your patio, or worse yet, your car, they can become a nuisance. If you have outdoor places you want to keep clean, avoid trees with large fruits (which make a big mess and attract yellow jackets), big and hard nuts or pods, and soft wooded trees that shed twigs and branches. Some nurseries carry neat alternatives for patios, walks, and driveway plantings—like fruit-free crabapples, seedless honey locusts, and fruitless (male) ginkgos.

DROPS TWIGS
River birch (*Betula nigra*)
Weeping willow (*Salix babylonica*)

NUTS, PODS, AND CONES
Hickories (*Carya* spp.)
Northern Catalpa (*Catalpa speciosa*)
Honey locust (*Gleditsia triacanthos*)
Kentucky coffee tree (*Gymnocladus dioica*)
Black walnut (*Juglans nigra*)
Sweet gum (*Liquidambar Styraciflua*)
Empress tree (*Paulowinia tomentosa*)
Sycamore (*Platanus occidentalis*)
Pines (*Pinus* spp.)
Cottonwood (*Populus deltoides*)
Black locust (*Robinia Pseudoacacia*)

FRUITS
Ginkgo (*Ginkgo biloba*)
Osage orange (*Maclura pomifera*)
Crabapples (large-fruited varieties) (*Malus* spp.)
Mulberry (*Morus* spp.)
Pears (*Pyrus communis*)
Plums (*Prunus* spp.)

TREES FOR EXPOSED, WINDY LOCATIONS

The Midwest is famous for its winds. In winter winds screaming off the Great Lakes lower wind chills to well below zero. In summer, stiff breezes can rapidly escalate to gales that can blow over newly planted trees. Winds can be fickle. A recent summer storm with dangerous tornadolike wind shears took out about half the Norway spruces in my Cleveland neighborhood, tipping them over, shallow roots and all. This same windstorm left the deep-rooted eastern white pines standing. To deal with wind, you've got to get tough. Break its velocity with stout, deep-rooted trees. Here are some possibilities.

Amur maple (*Acer Ginnala*)
Norway maple (*Acer platanoides*)
Red maple (*Acer rubrum*)
Sugar maple (*Acer saccharum*)
Tartarian maple (*Acer tataricum*)

Gray birch (*Betula populifolia*)
European hornbeam (*Carpinus Betulus*)
Ginkgo (*Ginkgo biloba*)
Thornless honey locust (*Gleditsia triacanthos* var. *inermis*)
Jack pine (*Pinus Banksiana*)
Austrian pine (*Pinus nigra*)
Red pine (*Pinus resinosa*)
Oaks (*Quercus* spp.)
Lindens (*Tilia* spp.)

TREES THAT RESEED MADLY

Preschoolers love to see the winged seeds of box elders and maples whirl down to the ground, spinning like helicopters. But to gardeners, this event spells trouble as young tree seedlings soon sprout in any patch of open ground. If allowed to get much past six inches tall, some tree seedlings can be so well anchored that they are nearly impossible to pull up. If cut off, they may resprout when your back is turned. Here are some of the most notorious.

Box elder (*Acer Negundo*)
Silver maple (*Acer saccharinum*)
Tree-of-heaven (*Ailanthus altissima*)
Gray birch (*Betula populifolia*)
Goldenrain tree (*Koelreuteria paniculata*)   White Poplar
White poplar (*Populus alba*)
Eastern cottonwood (*Populus deltoides*)

TREES WITH FRAGRANT BLOSSOMS

Fragrance has the power to lift spirits and beautify gardens without calling upon our most overused sense, vision. The size and color of the flower doesn't always reflect on the quality of aroma. Littleleaf linden trees, for instance, have tiny, dangling, yellow flowers that are difficult to see but easy to smell even from afar.

With eyes closed, the wafting fragrance of a fringe tree or crabapple in bloom can set the imagination wandering. Whenever you meet this aroma again, you will most probably remember it and even recall the warm sun on your back and the trilling of birds from the last time you caught the same elusive fragrance.

Fringe tree (*Chionanthus virginicus*)
Russian olive (*Elaeagnus angustifolia*)
Kentucky coffee tree (*Gymnocladus dioica*)
Sweet bay magnolia (*Magnolia virginiana*)
Crabapples (*Malus Sargentii*, M. *baccata*, M *coronaria*, 'Copper King',
        'Dolgo', and selected other species and cultivars)
Japanese flowering cherry (*Prunus serrulata*)
Black locust (*Robinia pseudoacacia*)
Littleleaf linden (*Tilia cordata*)

TREES FOR SOUTH CENTRAL KANSAS

Winter in South Central Kansas is characterized by fierce winds and little snow. Low temperatures may reach -10 degrees F—less frigid than more northern states, but because there is little or no insulating blanket of snow on the ground, plant loss can be high. Summer is just as tough, with droughts and blazing heat causing additional stress.

Despite these obstacles, there are some excellent trees for these kind of conditions, species that take a lickin' and keep on tickin'. Dr. John Pair, Research Horticulturist for Kansas State University, has conducted extensive field trials and found the following trees excelled under harsh conditions.

SMALL DECIDUOUS TREES TO 20 FEET
Amur maple (*Acer ginnala*)
Eastern redbud (*Cercis canadensis*)
Washington hawthorn (*Crataegus phaenopyrum*)
Flowering crabapple (*Malus* spp. 'Donald Wyman', 'Prairiefire', 'Snowdrift')

MEDIUM DECIDUOUS TREES TO 40 FEET
Shantung maple (*Acer truncatum*)
Goldenrain tree (*Koelreuteria paniculata*)
Osage orange (male thornless) (*Maclura pomifera*)
Callery pear (*Pyrus calleryana* 'Aristocrat', 'Chanticleer', 'Cleveland Select')
Sawtooth oak (*Quercus acutissima*)
Chestnut oak (*Quercus Muehlenbergii*)

LARGE DECIDUOUS TREES TO 60 FEET
Sugar maple (*Acer saccharum*)
River birch (*Betula nigra*)
White ash (*Fraxinus americana*)
Green ash (*Fraxinus pennsylvanica*)
Ginkgo (*Ginkgo biloba*)
Thornless honey locust (*Gleditsia triacanthos* var. *inermis*)
Swamp white oak (*Quercus bicolor*)
Shingle oak (*Quercus imbricaria*)
Lacebark elm (*Ulmus parvifolia*)

VERY LARGE DECIDUOUS TREES OVER 60 FEET
Bur oak (*Quercus macrocarpa*)
Shumard's red oak (*Quercus Shumardii*)
Bald cypress (*Taxodium distichum*)

EVERGREEN TREES
Upright Chinese juniper (*Juniperus chinensis*)
Black Hills spruce (*Picea glauca* 'Densata')
Pinyon pine (*Pinus cembroides* var. *edulis*)

"Great new trees are continually being introduced to the nursery industry. But they can take a long time to reach your local garden center. If you read about a new tree you simply must have, call your garden center and ask them to order it for you. If you wait for it to come into stock without prodding, years may pass before your tree arrives.

"There are always new introductions that deserve attention, and perhaps they will someday replace many of the recommended cultivars [in these lists]. For example, we are just now evaluating a number of promising new elm species and hybrids from the U.S. National Arboretum. Also, there are a number of interesting elm introductions from China (*Ulmus Davidiana, U. Wilsoniana*, and others) of special interest."

Dr. John Pair, researcher, Kansas State University

TREES FOR TOUGH URBAN SITES

City life can be grueling for trees. Rain rolls off acres of pavement into sewers without moistening the ground, beating sun superheats black asphalt or reflects blindingly off light cement. Air pollution causes sensitive foliage to brown out. What little exposed soil there is is walked on by pedestrians and polluted by dogs. Despite these difficult conditions, a few tree species can thrive, spreading soft green leaves and shade where it is needed most.

Expect to expend a little effort to get them going and tend them carefully during drought. Water, fertilizer, and protection from man and beast is a small price to pay for the luxury of a lovely tree in the cement jungle.

Amur maple (*Acer ginnala*)
Norway maple (*Acer platanoides*)
European hornbeam (*Carpinus Betulus*)
Common hackberry (*Celtis occidentalis*)
Nootka false cypress (*Chamaecyparis nootkatensis*)
Hawthorns (*Crataegus* spp.)
Russian olive (*Elaeagnus angustifolia*)
Green ash (*Fraxinus pennsylvanica*)
Ginkgo (*Ginkgo biloba*)
Common witch hazel (*Hamamelis virginiana*)
Panicled goldenrain tree (*Koelreuteria paniculata*)
Saucer magnolia (*Magnolia × soulangiana*)
Staghorn sumac (*Rhus typhina*)
Littleleaf linden (*Tilia cordata*)
Lacebark elm (*Ulmus parvifolia*)

TREES FOR AREAS TROUBLED WITH DEER

Across the Midwest, trees are mauled by hungry deer. Deer can go beyond delicate nibbling and devour trees or scrape off enough bark to create wounds beyond repair. Most evergreens are particularly at risk during the winter, when other food sources are limited. If even a few deer tend to pause in your yard, avoid planting their favorite foods and stick to trees they find less palatable.

FAVORITE TREES FOR DEER
Hawthorns (*Crataegus* spp.)
Crabapples (*Malus* spp.)
Mulberries (*Morus alba*)
Hemlocks (*Tsuga* spp.)

TREES DEER FIND LESS DELECTIBLE
Maples (*Acer* spp.)
Birches (*Betula* spp.)
Hornbeams (*Carpinus* spp.)
Redbuds (*Cercis* spp.)
Dogwoods (*Cornus* spp.)
Beeches (*Fagus* spp.)
Ashes (*Fraxinus* spp.)
Ginkgo (*Ginkgo biloba*)
Honey locust (*Gleditsia triacanthos*)
Larches (*Larix* spp.)
Sweet gum (*Liquidambar Styraciflua*)
Tulip tree (*Liriodendron Tulipifera*)
Sour gum (*Nyssa sylvatica*)
Sycamores (*Platanus* spp.)
Oaks (*Quercus* spp.)
Willows (*Salix* spp.)
Bald cypress (*Taxodium distichum*)

"The deer pressure is increasing in Lake County, Ohio, and we're seeing deer focus less on eating only their desired species. When there are enough deer, they'll eat anything! A most desired species used to be crabapples, but now they're going for pines and hemlocks too. Yews were favorites in the past, but now deer are also eating junipers and arborvitaes.

"In many native woodlands, we're losing the understory trees and shrubs because deer are nibbling off the terminal growth, buds, and young shoots. Taller trees are fairly safe, but even young ashes and maples should be protected. There have been a couple of sites where we kept deer out of wooded plots and found the understory plants made an amazing recovery. We surround protected areas with six- to eight-foot tall black plastic mesh fencing, and at least for the time being, it has kept deer away."

Peter Bristol, Director of Horticulture for Holden Arboretum, Painesville, Ohio

Trees through the Seasons

We may occasionally complain about the heat and the cold, but one advantage of living in the Midwest is a robust set of seasons. From a cheerful mild spring to a warm, luxurious summer, a cool and bright fall, and a long, quiet winter, there is constant change and interest in the landscape. Make the most of our seasons by planting trees that change through the year, from flowers to ornamental fruit or pods, interesting foliage to good autumn color, and handsome bark for winter displays. Ideas abound in the following lists.

DECIDUOUS TREES WITH UNUSUAL FOLIAGE COLOR

For dramatic foliage color during the growing season, consider using one or several of the following brightly clad trees. Match leaf color to nearby flowers or evergreens, the house, the curtains, or other prominent features for a finished, complementary color scheme. But when using colored foliage, remember it's possible to overdo; if every tree is gold or bronze, for example, the landscape can look gaudy or unnatural.

RED OR PURPLE AUTUMN FOLIAGE
Japanese maples (*Acer palmatum* var. *atropurpureum* 'Bloodgood', 'Burgandy Lace', 'Garnet', 'Red Filigree Lace', and others)
Norway maple (*Acer platanoides* 'Crimson King', 'Crimson Sentry', 'Royal Red', 'Faasens Black', and others)
Forest Pansy redbud (*Cercis canadensis* 'Forest Pansy')
European beech (*Fagus sylvatica* 'Atropunicea', 'Cuprea', 'Purpurea Pendula', 'Riversii', 'Roseo-marginata', 'Tricolor')
Crabapples (*Malus* spp. 'Brandywine', 'Candied Apple', 'Evelyn' [disease resistant], 'Liset', 'Profusion', 'Red Splendor', 'Royalty', 'Sunset', and more)
Cherry plum (*Prunus cerasifera* 'Atropurpurea', 'Newport Thundercloud')
Common chokecherry (*Prunus virginiana* 'Shubert', 'Canada Red')

GOLD OR VARIEGATED AUTUMN FOLIAGE
Norway maple (*Acer platanoides* 'Aureo-marginatum')
Sycamore maple (*Acer pseudoplatanus* f. *variegatum*)
Tricolor dogwood (*Cornus florida* 'Welchii')
Cherokee Chief dogwood (*Cornus florida* 'Cherokee Chief')
Variegated European beech (*Fagus sylvatica* 'Albo-variegata', 'Luteo-variegata')
Sunburst honey locust (*Gleditsia triacanthos inermis* 'Sunburst')
Gold Dust sweet gum (*Liquidambar Styraciflua* 'Gold Dust')
Gold Crown linden (*Tilia* spp. 'Gold Crown')

BLUE, GRAY, WHITE, OR SILVER AUTUMN FOLIAGE
Drummond Norway maple (*Acer rubrum* var. *'Drummondii'*)
Russian olive (*Elaeagnus angustifolia*)
Tschonoskii's crabapple (*Malus Tschonoskii*)
Silver Frost pear (*Pyrus salicifolia pendula* 'Silfrozam')

TREES FOR EVERGREEN APPEAL

Like a colorized version of a black and white movie, evergreens bring a little sparkle to long, gray Midwestern winters—and in this small act comes merit beyond measure. They also provide unfaltering privacy, screen out unwanted views, and help to muffle loud neighborhood noises. Many evergreen trees have a conical shape that can provide a formal look if tightly sheared. Others, such as the black pine (*Pinus nigra*), if allowed to grow unclipped, will widen into picturesque open shapes reminiscent of the sculpted pines in Japanese gardens.

Firs (*Abies* spp.)
American holly (*Ilex opaca*)
Upright junipers (*Juniperus* spp.)
Spruces (*Picea* spp.)
Pines (*Pinus* spp.)
Canadian hemlock (*Tsuga canadensis*)

EVERGREEN TREES WITH VARYING FOLIAGE COLORS

Evergreen trees with foliage tinted with blue or gold tones assume great prominence in the winter landscape.

Blue Evergreen Foliage
Baker blue spruce (*Picea pungens* 'Bakeri')
Colorado blue spruce (*Picea pungens* 'Glauca')

Gold Evergreen Foliage
Golden threadleaf false cypress (*Chamaecyparis pisifera* 'Filifera Aurea')
Gold Cargo arborvitae (*Thuja occidentalis* 'Gold Cargo')

JEFF FORINASH'S FAVORITE NEW CONIFERS

Gerard Nursery, located in Geneva, Ohio, grows a great assortment of conifers ideal for Midwestern gardens. Propagator Jeff Forinash has gone out on a limb to predict the following new evergreen trees will be rising stars of future gardens. Newer and better cultivars, they are easy to grow and endowed with handsome form and great foliage color. Among them, you'll find tall and compact sizes, upright and spreading shapes, and personalities suitable for mixing into a garden bed or highlighting as a lone specimen.

Compact Rocky mountain fir (*Abies lasiocarpa* 'Compacta')
Aurea Korean fir (*Abies koreana* 'Aurea')
Prostrate Beauty Korean fir (*Abies koreana* 'Prostrate Beauty')
Pendulous Nootka false cypress (*Chamaecyparis nootkatensis* 'Pendula')
Acrocona Norway spruce (*Picea Abies* 'Acrocona')
Jane Kluis Japanese red pine (*Pinus densiflora* 'Jane Kluis')
Wee Rogue limber pine (*Pinus flexilis* 'Wee Rogue')
Silver Ray Korean pine (*Pinus koraiensis* 'Silver Ray')
Fuku Zu Mi Japanese white pine (*Pinus parviflora* 'Fuku Zu Mi')
Bergman Japanese white pine (*Pinus parviflora* 'Bergman')
Greg's Broom white pine (*Pinus strobus* 'Greg's Broom')

Riverside Gem Scotch pine (*Pinus sylvestris* 'Riverside Gem')
Prostrate Scotch pine (*Pinus sylvestris* 'Albyns Prostrata')
Veridis Scotch pine (*Pinus sylvestris* 'Veridis')
Spring Frost Canadian hemlock (*Tsuga canadensis* 'Spring Frost')

DISCOVERING NEW CULTIVARS

"Girard Nursery has display gardens with over three thousand trees in different settings, which is a great way for people to discover and get excited about new conifers. People see these new conifers, find out what they can do in the garden, like them, and want them. We also have addicted *coniferiles* who are always browsing around here looking for something new and are excited to find these offerings."

Jeff Forinash, propagator for Girard Nursery

TREES THAT ATTRACT BIRDS AND BUTTERFLIES

Trees are like high-rise apartments for birds, colorful and lively garden visitors. Some trees have nectar-rich flowers—the main course for hummingbirds—or nutritious pods, nuts, and berries—hors d'oeuvres for fruit and seed eaters like chickadees and goldfinches. Leafy limbs also offer shelter, nesting sites, and shade. The following trees top the list for attracting birds; they should be planted away from outdoor entertaining or sitting areas lest someone be unpleasantly surprised from above.

BIRD-ATTRACTING TREES

Maples (*Acer* spp.)
Shadblow (*Amelanchier canadensis*)
River birch (*Betula nigra*)
Hackberry (*Celtis occidentalis*)
Fringe tree (*Chionanthus virginicus*)
Dogwoods (*Cornus* spp.)
Hawthorns (*Crataegus* spp.)
Crabapples (*Malus* spp.)
Mulberry (*Morus* spp.)
Black gum (*Nyssa sylvatica*)
Spruces (*Picea* spp.)
White pine (*Pinus strobus*)
Mountain ash (*Sorbus* spp.)

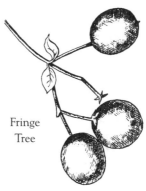

Fringe
Tree

HUMMINGBIRD-ATTRACTING TREES

Red and bright pink flowers draw hummingbirds like a magnet, but they will also come to flowers of other colors if they contain rich supplies of nectar. For the most successful hummingbird garden, plant hummingbird-attracting trees, shrubs, and flowers that bloom in succession through the entire growing season.

Red buckeye (*Aesculus Pavia*)
Hawthorns (*Crataegus* spp.)
Tulip poplar (*Liriodendron Tulipifera*)
Crabapples (*Malus* spp.)
Cherries and plums (*Prunus* spp.)
Black locust (*Robinia pseudoacacia*)

SAMPLER OF TREES BY COLOR OF FLOWERS AND SEASON

For flowering trees, there is no time like springtime, when their blossoms play colorful duets with flowering shrubs and bulbs. The most reliable flowering trees open once frost is past. Earlier bloomers are precious, but cold snaps may cut short their flowers. Although more limited in number, you also should seek out later bloomers, ideal for underplanting with annual and perennial flowers of complementary colors.

This survey of flower color and bloom time is a general guide to help plan color schemes in the garden. You may have to modify it to fit your particular combination of cultivars, climate, and site factors.

WHITE FLOWERS

Serviceberry (*Amelanchier* spp.)	Spring
Fringe tree (*Chionanthus virginicus*)	Spring/Summer
Flowering dogwood (*Cornus florida*)	Spring
Chinese dogwood (*Cornus Kousa*)	Early summer
Smoke tree (*Cotinus Coggygria*)	Summer
Hawthorn (*Crataegus* spp.)	Spring
Magnolias (*Magnolia* spp.)	Spring
Crabapples (*Malus* spp.)	Spring
Cherries (*Prunus* spp.)	Spring
Japanese pagoda tree (*Sophora japonica*)	Late summer
Mountain ash (*Sorbus* spp.)	Spring
Japanese Stewartia (*Stewartia pseudocamellia*)	Summer
Japanese snowbell (*Styrax japonicus*)	Late spring
Japanese tree lilac (*Syringa reticulata*)	Late spring

BLUE OR VIOLET FLOWERS

Purple smoke tree (*Cotinus Coggygria* 'Velvet Cloak')	Summer

YELLOW FLOWERS

Cornelian cherry (*Cornus mas*)	Early spring
Chinese witch hazel (*Hamamelis mollis*)	Early spring
Witch hazel (*Hamamelis virginiana*)	Fall
Goldenrain tree (*Koelreuteria paniculata*)	Summer
Golden-chain tree (*Laburnum × Watereri*)	Spring
Tulip tree (*Liriodendron Tulipifera*)	Spring
Magnolia hybrids (*Magnolia* hyb.)	Spring

PINK/LAVENDER FLOWERS

Redbud (*Cercis canadensis*)	Spring
Pink flowering dogwood (*Cornus florida*)	Spring
Pink crabapples (*Malus* hyb.)	Spring
Magnolias (*Magnolia* spp.)	Spring
Cherries (*Prunus* spp.)	Spring

RED FLOWERS

Red maple (*Acer rubrum*)	Early spring

Red buckeye (*Aesculus Pavia*)	Spring
Red crabapples (*Malus* hyb.)	Spring

YELLOW MAGNOLIAS FOR A NEW AGE
   "One of the greatest new accomplishments of tree-breeding programs is the new yellow-flowered magnolias, hybrids of the cucumber magnolia (*Magnolia acuminata*) and the Chinese porcelain magnolia (*M. denudata*).
   "Some of the current best are 'Elizabeth' and 'Butterflies'. They flower before the leaves open, creating a wonderful show, and are hardy into Zone 4. There may be hundreds of new varieties in the next twenty years because of all the great breeding work being done right now."
   Roy Klehm, from Klehm's Nursery, Champaign, Illinois

A SAMPLER OF TREES BY THEIR FALL COLOR

For a delightful end to the growing season, consider painting a beautiful fall picture with blends of different colored autumn foliage. Here are some examples of trees to intermingle with richly colored shrubs, evergreens, late-blooming perennials, and the final hurrahs of annuals. With sunny autumn days and cool nights, these trees take on the most vivid colors; during wetter than usual autumns, their colors may be more muted.

Maples (*Acer* spp.)	Red to yellow
Serviceberry (*Amelanchier* spp.)	Red to yellow
Birches (*Betula* spp.)	Yellow
Hornbeam (*Carpinus* spp.)	Yellow to red
Katsura tree (*Cercidiphyllum japonicum*)	Orange to yellow
Redbud (*Cercis canadensis*)	Yellow
Yellowwood (*Cladrastis lutea*)	Yellow
Dogwoods (*Cornus* spp.)	Red
Hawthorn (*Crataegus* spp.)	Orange
European beech (*Fagus sylvatica*)	Bronze
White ash (*Fraxinus americana*)	Yellow to maroon
Franklin tree (*Franklinia Altamaha*)	Orange
Ginkgo (*Ginkgo biloba*)	Yellow
Honey locust (*Gleditsia triacanthos* var. *inermis*)	Yellow
Kentucky coffee tree (*Gymnocladus dioica*)	Yellow
Panicled goldenrain tree (*Koelreuteria paniculata*)	Yellow
Japanese larch (*Larix Kaempferi*)	Yellow
Sweet gum (*Liquidambar Styraciflua*)	Yellow to maroon
Tulip tree (*Liriodendron Tulipifera*)	Yellow
Black gum (*Nyssa sylvatica*)	Orange red
American hop hornbeam (*Ostrya virginiana*)	Yellow
Sourwood (*Oxydendrum arboreum*)	Red
Red oak (*Quercus rubra*)	Red
Sassafras (*Sassafras albidum*)	Orange
Little leaf linden (*Tilia cordata*)	Yellow to red
Elms (*Ulmus* spp.)	Yellow

TREES WITH ORNAMENTAL BERRIES FOR SUMMER OR FALL

For extra color after the flowers are long gone, the following trees offer bright berries that sometimes persist well into winter.

Serviceberry (*Amelanchier* spp.)	Red	Summer
Dogwoods (*Cornus* spp.)	Red	Summer/Fall
Hawthorns (*Crataegus* spp.)	Red	Fall
American holly (*Ilex opaca*)	Red	Fall/Winter
Crabapples (*Malus* spp.)	Red/Yellow	Fall/Winter
Mountain ash (*Sorbus* spp.)	Orange/Red	Summer/Fall
Sumacs (*Rhus* spp.)	Red	Summer/Fall/Winter

TREES WITH SHOWY BARK COLOR, TEXTURE, OR PATTERN

More subtle displays of handsome bark take on a new excitement when uncloaked by winter. Some of the more flamboyantly barked trees, like the paperbark maple (*Acer griseum*), also hold their own in summer. If choosing between two trees and all other qualities are equal, plant the tree with the most graceful, colorful, or interesting bark, using the list below as your guide.

Paperbark maple (*Acer griseum*)
Japanese maple (*Acer palmatum*)
Serviceberry (*Amelanchier* spp.)
Birches (*Betula* spp.)
Shagbark hickory (*Carya ovata*)
American beech (*Fagus grandifolia*)
Franklin tree (*Franklinia altamaha*)
Lacebark pine (*Pinus Bungeana*)

Shagbark
Hickory

London plane tree (*Platanus × acerifolia*)
Sycamore (*Platanus occidentalis*)
Golden Curls and Scarlet Curls willow ('Golden Curls', 'Scarlet Curls')
Lacebark elm (*Ulmus parvifolia*)

CAROLYN STROOMBEEKS'S FAVORITE TREES WITH EXFOLIATING BARK

Some trees have artistic exfoliating bark with surface grays or browns that peel away to reveal a different colored bark below. The best known exfoliating Midwestern tree is the sycamore with its reddish-brown bark peeling back to display white beneath. Sycamores, which grow nicely in wooded floodplains, are not, however, ideal shade trees because of their litter and seed pods. To enjoy specimens of more controlled exfoliation in your yard, take a tip from Carolyn Stroombeek, plant collector and nurserywoman from wholesale Roemer Nursery in Madison, Ohio. Having experimented widely with exfoliating trees, Strombeek has found the following species to be best for the average homeowner.

Paperbark maple (*Acer griseum*)
Three flower maple (*Acer triflorum*)
White-barked Himalayan birch (*Betula Jacquemontii*)
Oriental fringe tree (*Chionanthus retusus*)
Japanese dogwood (*Cornus Kousa*)
Persian parrotia (*Parrotia persica*)
Lacebark pine (*Pinus Bungeana*)
Korean Stewartia (*Stewartia pseudocamellia*)
Chinese elm (*Ulmus parvifolia*)

Trees in the Landscape

Trees are not limited to those big, sturdy fellows that spread their arms over the yard and cast their shade about. In smaller yards and gardens, small trees fit in well when mixed with shrubs and flowers. Small trees often have multiple trunks, twining branches, and interesting shapes that can be used as landscape focal points, as interesting as any sculpture.

FAST-GROWING TREES

Where new yards stretch back to back as far as the eye can see, fast-growing trees can be called upon to frame the yard, cast shade, and provide privacy. Fast growers can grow from one to several feet per year, making their mark on the landscape in record time. But many (especially those marked with an asterisk) are troubled by soft, weak wood—the price paid for rapid growth. They can drop limbs or suffer split or broken trunks when the weather becomes severe, or they may die at a young age from insect or disease damage.

*Tree-of-heaven (*Ailanthus altissima*)
*Box elder (*Acer Negundo*)
 Red maple (*Acer rubrum*)
*Silver maple (*Acer saccharinum*)
 River birch (*Betula nigra*)
 Green ash (*Fraxinus pennsylvanica*)
 Goldenrain tree (*Koelreuteria paniculata*)
 Sweet gum (*Liquidambar Styraciflua*)
 Tulip poplar (*Liriodendron Tulipifera*)
 Sycamore (*Platanus occidentalis*)
*White poplar (*Populus alba*)
*Cottonwood (*Populus deltoides*)
*Bradford Callery pear (*Pyrus calleryana* 'Bradford')
 Scarlet oak (*Quercus coccinea*)
 Pin oak (*Quercus palustris*)
*Weeping willow (*Salix babylonica*)
 Bald cypress (*Taxodium distichum*)
 Lacebark elm (*Ulmus parvifolia*)
 Japanese Zelkova (*Zelkova serrata*)

 An ideal garden plan blends fast-growing trees for quick cover with slow-growing trees. Once the slow growers reach an impressive size, you can remove the weaker trees.

COMPACT TREES FOR SMALL YARDS, MIXED BEDS, OR PATIO PLANTINGS

Instead of billowing over a large portion of the yard, small trees keep more to themselves, working nicely in a compact bed, patio planter, or courtyard. You can surround them with flowers or shrubs, creating layered plantings of interest from top to bottom. Some of the following trees are naturally compact; others are more petite cultivars of full-sized trees.

> Amur maple (*Acer ginnala*)
> Laceleaf Japanese maple (*Acer palmatum* 'Dissectum')
> Serviceberry 'Spring Glory' (*Amelanchier canadensis* 'Spring Glory')
> Chinese dogwood 'Milky Way' (*Cornus Kousa* 'Milky Way')
> Hawthorns, compact cultivars (*Crataegus inermis* 'Crusader',
>   *Crataegus crus-galli*)
> Russian olive (*Elaeagnus angustifolia*)
> Weeping purple European beech (*Fagus sylvatica* 'Purpurea Pendula')
> Franklin tree (*Franklinia altamaha*)
> Magnolias Ann and Betty (*Magnolia* × 'Ann'; M. × 'Betty')
> Star magnolia (*Magnolia stellata*)
> Sweet bay magnolia (*Magnolia virginiana*)
> Crabapples (*Malus* spp.)
> Flowering cherries, weeping and compact cultivars (*Prunus serrulata*)
> Newport cherry plum (*Prunus* × *cerasifera* 'Newport')

TREES WITH MULTIPLE TRUNKS

Multi-trunked trees tend to be more compact and broad spreading than the same tree with a single trunk. Their graceful silhouettes are almost an art form in themselves. Ask a local nursery if they carry multiple trunked forms of the following trees. (More multiple trunked small trees can be found in the chapter on shrubs.)

> Hedge maple (*Acer campestre*)
> Japanese maple (*Acer palmatum*)
> Paperbark maple (*Acer griseum*)
> Amur maple (*Acer ginnala*)
> River birch (*Betula nigra*)
> American hornbeam (*Carpinus caroliniana*)
> Flowering dogwood (*Cornus florida*)
> Carolina silverbell (*Halesia carolina*)
> Flowering magnolias (*Magnolia* spp.)
> Asian white birch (*Betula platyphylla* 'White Spire')
> Sergeant crabapple (*Malus Sargentii*)
> Persian parrotia (*Parrotia persica*)
> Lacebark pine (*Pinus Bungeana*)
> Japanese snowbell (*Styrax japonica*)
> Japanese Stewartia (*Stewartia pseudocamellia*)

SPECIAL TREE FORMS FOR DESIGNS

Sometimes a certain place in the yard cries out for a spreading tree, one that softens upright walls and buildings. In other areas, a graceful vase-shaped tree, which arcs upward and outward like a fountain, provides the perfect touch. In other places—tight on space or in need of a formal accent—only an upright tree will do. Here are some different tree shapes to mix and match to special sites around the yard.

VASE-SHAPED SHADE TREES

Japanese maple (*Acer palmatum*)
Yellowwood (*Cladrastris lutea*)
Honey locust (*Gleditsia triacanthos*)
Red oak (*Quercus rubra*)
Japanese pagoda tree (*Sophora japonica*)
Japanese Stewartia (*Stewartia pseudocamellia*)
American elm (*Ulmus americana*, disease resistant forms such as
    'Delaware #2' and 'Washington')
Lacebark elm (*Ulmus parviflora*)
Japanese Zelkova (*Zelkova serrata*)

INTERESTING AND UNUSUAL SHAPES

Novel twists and turns in branches, twigs, or trunks of the following list of trees provide eye-catching highlights in the yards of adventurous souls and in places that cry out for attention.

Contorted filbert (*Corylus Avellana* 'Controta')
Teas weeping mulberry (*Morus alba* 'Pendula')
Contorted mulberry (*Morus bombycis* 'Unryu')
Dragon-claw willow (*Salix Matsudana* 'Tortuosa')

WEEPING TREES

Nothing is more likely to bring a sigh of appreciation from garden guests than a weeping cherry in full bloom—people travel all the way to Japan for this impressive sight. Weeping trees help soften corners and break up visually tight clusters of rounded shrubs and mounded perennials. Not all weeping trees achieve their graceful shape naturally; some, like weeping cherries, are rare weeping branched clones grafted onto upright trunks. (The botanical names of weeping cultivars often include the word *pendula*, in reference to their pendulous branches.)

Deciduous Weeping Trees
Weeping Katsura tree (*Cercidiphyllum japonicum* 'Pendula')
Weeping European beech (*Fagus sylvatica* 'Pendula')
Weeping purple European beech (*Fagus sylvatica* 'Purpurea Pendula')
Weeping larch (*Larix decidua* 'Pendula')
Weeping crabapples (*Malus* spp. 'Molten Lava', 'Red Jade',
    'Weeping Candied Apple')
Weeping mulberry (*Morus alba* 'Chaparral', 'Pendula')
Weeping higan cherry (*Prunus subhirtella* 'Pendula', 'Pendula Plena Rosea')

Snow Fountains flowering cherry (*Prunus* × 'Snow Fountains')
Weeping willowleaf pear (*Pyrus salicifolia pendula* and 'Silfrozam')
Golden weeping willow (*Salix alba* 'Tristis')
Weeping willow (*Salix babylonica*)
Thurlow weeping willow (*Salix* × *elegantissima*)
Weeping scotch elm (*Ulmus glabra* 'Camperdownii', 'Pendula')

Evergreen Weeping Trees
Weeping Norway spruce (*Picea Abies forma* 'Pendula')
Weeping Serbian spruce (*Picea Omorika* 'Pendula')
Weeping Limber pine (*Pinus flexilis* 'Pendula')
Weeping white pine (*Pinus strobus* 'Pendula')
Sergeant's weeping hemlock (*Tsuga canadensis* 'Pendula Sargentii')

HORIZONTAL BRANCHING FOR THE LAYERED LOOK

Like a view across a prairie or Lake Erie at sunset, horizontal horizons are naturally beautiful. In landscapes where trunks, fence posts, lamps, and utility poles all rise starkly upward, horizontal branches provide welcome diversity. The elegantly layered shadowy depths of a tree canopy can be downright spectacular. Here are some special trees gifted with distinctive horizontal branching habits.

Japanese maple (*Acer palmatum*)
Redbud (*Cercis canadensis*)
Pagoda dogwood (*Cornus alternifolia*)
Flowering dogwood (*Cornus florida*)
Cockspur hawthorn (*Crataegus crus-galli*)
Washington hawthorn (*Crataegus phaenopyrum*)
European beech (*Fagus sylvatica*)
Japanese flowering crabapple (*Malus Floribunda*)
Japanese snowbell (*Styrax japonica*)

COLUMNAR, UPRIGHT TREES FOR NARROW SPACES

Because most trees spread their arms wide and embrace the yard, those that stand strictly upright will always grab attention. They can be sentinels beside doorways or gates or emphatic counterpoints to mounded or low-growing shrubs and flowers. (When dense, upright evergreens are used in snowy climates, wrap them in burlap to prevent winter damage.)

Green column black maple (*Acer nigrum* 'Greencolumn')
Columnar Norway maple (*Acer platanoides* 'Columnare', 'Erectum')
Columnar red maple (*Acer rubrum* 'Columnare', 'Armstrong')
Endowment sugar maple (*Acer saccharum* 'Endowment')
Spartan juniper (*Juniperus chinensis* 'Spartan')
Skyrocket juniper (*Juniperus scopulorum* 'Skyrocket')
Columnar crabapples (*Malus* 'Centurion', 'Excalibur',
    'Harvest Gold', 'Lancelot', 'Madonna', 'Red Barron', 'Sentinel',
    'Velvet Pillar', and more)
Upright European aspen (*Populus tremula* 'Erecta')

Amanogawa Japanese flowering cherry (*Prunus serrulata* 'Amanogawa')
Chanticleer or Cleveland Select Callery pear (*Pyrus calleryana* 'Chanticleer')
Whitehouse Callery pear (*Pyrus calleryana* 'White House')
Fastigiata English oak (*Quercus robur* 'Fastigiata')

SHRUBS

Shrubs are an exceptionally variable and versatile group of plants. Consider the juniper. Creeping junipers like 'New Blue' and golden 'Mother Lode' are spreading evergreen ground covers. Low-growing junipers like the thirty-inch high 'Saybrook Gold' or 'Blue Danube' form compact mounds that fit in well with flowers or herbs in formal or informal gardens, borders, or island beds. Taller, bushier junipers like 'Gold Coast' and 'Sea Green' can go into a foundation planting, while the six-foot high hetz blue juniper (*Juniperus chinensis* 'Hetzii Glauca') makes a great privacy hedge in the backyard. Upright junipers, tall and slim like 'Skyrocket' or pyramid-shaped like 'Hooks', can stand at attention at either side of a doorway.

Plants don't always follow the rules we set up for them, and this is the case with shrubs that double as small trees. Shrubs are defined as woody-stemmed plants having multiple main stems or trunks. Many classic shrubs, like viburnums and lilacs, have dozens of small- to medium-sized stems sprouting from the ground. Other shrubs may have a only a few larger trunks, as is the case with witch hazels (which can be classed as either a shrub or a small tree), or a shrub can be pruned to a few main trunks and used as a small tree, as are some lilacs. Small upright evergreens are included in the shrub category, even though they may only have one main trunk, because they do the work of shrubs in the landscape.

Formal hedges are usually clipped or sheared into a specific geometric shape, but most shrubs do not require regular shearing. Shearing actually accelerates their growth rate and makes it harder to maintain a shrub at a specific size. Instead of doctoring up overly large shrubs, select a shrub cultivar that is the proper size for the job at hand. Save your pruning shears for trimming off old flowers or removing dead or awkward branches.

Before you buy, do a little homework to find the best shrub for the site and purpose. The following lists will help you get started.

Right Plant, Right Place

As with any plant group, there are shrubs that thrive in sun or shade or moist or dry soil so determine what conditions your garden site offers and select shrubs accordingly. If you live in a windy area—in Euclid on the blustery Lake Erie shore, for instance—look for shrubs well-suited for exposed sites. In small gardens like those beautiful, postcard-sized yards in the German Village area of Columbus, Ohio, avoid shrubs that spread quickly or qualify as invasive. These same vigorous growers, however, may be just the answer for a forlorn slope or a larger garden.

SHRUBS FOR DRY SOILS

Sandy, rapidly draining soils, found in small pockets in northwest Indiana and along the Lake Erie shore in metropolitan Cleveland, are easy to plant in spring but you'll pay the price for that convenience later. When summer heat and drought hit, they become parched—a condition that can spell the end for moisture lovers like rhododendrons. For these areas, well-drained hillsides, or places you can't water easily, plant shrubs that aren't bothered by dry soils. Even the most durable species will need some deep watering for as much as a year after planting to encourage new roots to dig down to where the soil stays moist and cool. Adding organic material to these soils will help build up their water-holding capacity and expand the number of shrubs you can grow.

Five-leaf aralia (*Acanthopanax Sieboldianus*)
Chokecherry (*Aronia arbutifolia*)
Barberries (*Berberis* spp.)
Butterfly bush (*Buddleia Davidii*)
Flowering quince (*Chaenomeles speciosa*)
Smokebush (*Cotinus Coggygria*)
Cotoneasters (*Cotoneaster* spp.)
Scotch broom (*Cytisus scoparius*)
Russian olive (*Elaegnus angustifolia*)
Forsythia (*Forsythia* × *intermedia*)
Junipers (*Juniperus* spp.)
Beautybush (*Kolkwitzia amabilis*)
Privet (*Ligustrum* spp.)
Bayberry (*Myrica pensylvanica*)
Potentilla (*Potentilla* spp.)
Fire thorn (*Pyracantha coccinea*)
Sumac (*Rhus* spp.)
Alpine currant (*Ribes alpinum*)
Rugosa rose (*Rosa rugosa*)
Common snowberry (*Symphoricarpos albus* and hybrids)
Wayfaring tree viburnum (*Viburnum lantana*)
Nannyberry viburnum (*Viburnum Lentago*)
Black haw viburnum (*Viburnum prunifolium*)
Yucca (*Yucca filamentosa*)

SHRUBS FOR MODERATE TO DEEP SHADE

Where tall shade trees reign or buildings cast long shadows, roses and sun-loving flowers fail but shade tolerant shrubs grow merrily. For maximum enjoyment, look for shrubs with white or light pastel flowers or variegated markings on the foliage that seem to glow in the waning light. Where shade is particularly deep and root competition with shallow-rooted shade trees is intense, even the toughest shrubs may flounder, flowering minimally if at all and growing scant and lanky. Should this happen, have an arborist thin out overcrowded overhead tree limbs, irrigate, and apply extra fertilizer to reduce competition between dueling root systems.

Red chokeberry (*Aronia arbutifolia*)
Five-leaf aralia (*Acanthopanax Sieboldianus*)
Common sweetshrub (*Calycanthus floridus*)
Summer-sweet clethra (*Clethra alnifolia*)
Gray dogwood (*Cornus racemosa*)
Red-osier dogwood (*Cornus sericea*)
Wintercreeper euonymus(*Euonymus Fortunei*)
Common witch hazel (*Hamamelis virginiana*)
Virginia sweetspire (*Itea virginica*)
Privet (*Ligustrum* spp.)
Spicebush (*Lindera Benzoin*)
Black jetbead (*Rhodotypos scandens*)
Alpine currant (*Ribes alpinum*)
Yews (*Taxus* spp.)
Snowberry (*Symphoricarpos* spp.)
Leatherleaf viburnum (*Viburnum rhytidophyllum*)

Sweetshrub

SHRUBS THAT TOLERATE LIGHT SHADE

Where the illumination of a site is halfway between sun and shade, try these high performers. Most of the shrubs listed under Shrubs for Moderate to Deep Shade also grow well here.

Glossy abelia (*Abelia* × *grandiflora*)
Korean beautyberry (*Callicarpa dichotoma*)
Beautyberry (*Callicarpa americana*)
Sweet pepperbush (*Clethra alnifolia*)
Dwarf fothergilla (*Fothergilla Gardenii*)
Hills-of-snow (*Hydrangea arborescens* 'Grandiflora')
French hydrangea (*Hydrangea macrophylla*)
Oak leaf hydrangea (*Hydrangea quercifolia*)
Japanese kerria (*Kerria japonica*)
Honeysuckle (*Lonicera* spp.)
Viburnum (*Viburnum* spp.)

ERICACEOUS SHRUBS FOR LIGHT SHADE

The following shrubs are ideal for light shade but insist on acidic, humus-rich, well-drained but evenly moist soil. If your garden naturally fills this bill, or if you don't mind creating and maintaining this special environment with soil amendments, you can enjoy the following shrubs.

Mountain

Mountain laurel (*Kalmia latifolia*)
Leucothoe (*Leucothoe Fontanesiana*)
Oregon grape holly (*Mahonia Aquifolium*)
Azaleas and rhododendrons (*Rhododendron* spp.)
Blueberries (*Vaccinium* spp.)

SHRUBS FOR MOIST SOIL

Few shrubs, with the exception of some willows, will tolerate standing water for long, but quite a few thrive in uniformly moist soils. If you have a low place in the yard where moss grows better than grass or a pond, creek, or drainage ditch where cattails or equisetum thrive, consider the following moisture-loving shrubs.

Bog rosemary (*Andromeda Polifolia*)
Red chokecherry (*Aronia arbutifolia*)
Sweet shrub (*Calycanthus floridus*)
Summer-sweet clethra (*Clethra alnifolia*)
Tartarian dogwood (*Cornus alba*)
Gray dogwood (*Cornus racemosa*)
Red-osier dogwood (*Cornus sericea*)
Winterberry holly (*Ilex verticillata*)
Virginia sweetspire (*Itea virginica*)
Willows (*Salix* spp.)
Snowberry (*Symphoricarpos* spp.)

SHRUBS THAT CAN BECOME INVASIVE

In big yards, a large, impressive shrub that rambles into a magnificent thicket might be just the thing to make an impression or set some boundaries. But in smaller yards, these same shrubs may prove overwhelming.

Bottlebrush buckeye (*Aesculus parviflora*)
Gray dogwood (*Cornus racemosa*)
Blood-twig dogwood (*Cornus sanguinea*)
Red-osier dogwood (*Cornus sericea*)
Sumacs (*Rhus* spp.)
Streamco purple osier willow (*Salix purpurea* 'Streamco')
American elder (*Sambucus canadensis*)

SHRUBS LESS ATTRACTIVE TO DEER

There's no sense in buying a pricey shrub just to have it consumed by hungry herds of deer. Where these jackrabbits-on-hooves consistently browse, avoid their favorites: mountain laurels, euonymus, hollies, rhododendrons, roses, yews, and arborvitaes. Add to this list yourself by noting which neighborhood plants have been hardest hit. The deer populations near my house don't seem interested in viburnums, spirea, or my junipers. (There is, however, plenty of other food in open woodlands and meadows nearby, and my large dog, who'd like nothing more than to chase a deer, stands watch over these shrubs.)

Barberry (*Berberis* spp.)
Boxwood (*Buxus* spp.)
Summer-sweet clethra (*Clethra alnifolia*)
Cotoneasters (*Cotoneaster* spp.)
Smokebush (*Cotinus* spp.)
Scotch broom (*Cytisus* spp.)
Forsythia (*Forsythia* spp.)
Hydrangeas (*Hydrangea* spp.)
Inkberry holly (*Ilex glabra*)
Junipers (*Juniperus* spp. except *J. horizontalis*)
Japanese kerria (*Kerria japonica*)
Leucothoe (*Leucothoe Fontanesiana*)
Privet (*Ligustrum* spp.)
Spicebush (*Lindera Benzoin*)
Honeysuckle (*Lonicera* spp.)
Oregon grape holly (*Mahonia Aquifolium*)
Bayberry (*Myrica pensylvanica*)
Mock orange (*Philadelphus* spp.)
Japanese andromeda (*Pieris japonica*)
Potentilla (*Potentilla* spp.)
Pyracantha (*Pyracantha* spp.)
Spirea (*Spiraea* spp.)
Snowberries (*Symphoricarpos* spp.)
Lilacs (*Syringa* spp.)
Viburnums (*Viburnum* spp.)
Weigelas (*Weigela* spp.)

"While virtually extirpated in many areas early in this century, whitetail numbers now exceed fifteen million across the country. Some states, including New York, Pennsylvania, New Jersey, Florida, Ohio, and Illinois, have seen dramatic population increases, particularly during the past ten years."

Paul Curtis, Cornell Cooperative Extension, and Mila Richmond, New York Cooperative Fish and Wildlife Research Unit, taken from Reducing Deer Damage to Home Gardens and Landscape Plantings, *Department of Natural Resources, Cornell University, Ithaca, New York*

SHRUBS FREQUENTLY SEVERELY DAMAGED BY DEER

Cornell University's manual on deer control, a good little reference guide for the deer-troubled, recommends avoiding the following shrubs.

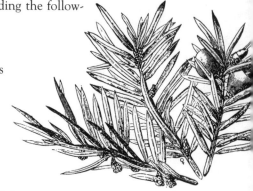

English Yew

Winged euonymus (*Euonymus alata*)
Rhododendrons and evergreen azaleas
    particularly 'Catawba' and
    'Pinxterbloom' (*Rhododendron*
    spp.)
English yew (*Taxus baccata*)
Western yew (*Taxus brevifolia*)
English/Japanese hybrid yew
    (*Taxus* × *media*)
American arborvitae (*Thuja occidentalis*)

TENACIOUS SHRUBS FOR BANKS AND SLOPES

Wherever your property suddenly takes a dive beside a steam, ditch, or steep hill, mowing becomes a chore and erosion creates even more problems. Rather than trying to maintain grass on steep slopes, call upon an elite group of shrubs to blanket the bank. Shrubs with vigorous root systems or graceful cascading limbs that root as they grow, can replace lawn or barren clay. But they need a little help to get off to a good start. Make *planting pockets*, level planting areas with a built up rim of soil at the perimeter, to help hold moisture while new shrubs get going. Pamper them until they are growing strongly and filling out the slope.

Gray, blood-twig, and red-osier dogwoods (*Cornus* spp.)
Cranberry cotoneaster (*Cotoneaster apiculata*)
Creeping cotoneaster (*Cotoneaster adpressus*)
Bearberry cotoneaster (*Cotoneaster Dammeri*)
Rockspray cotoneaster (*Cotoneaster horizontalis*)
Wintercreeper euonymus (*Euonymus Fortunei*)
Weeping forsythia (*Forsythia suspensa* var. *Sieboldii*)
Shrubby St. John's wort (*Hypericum prolificum*)
Creeping juniper (*Juniperus horizontalis*)
Japgarden juniper (*Juniperus chinensis* var. *Procumbens*)
Blue Carpet single-seed juniper (*Juniperus squamata*)
Northern bayberry (*Myrica pensylvanica*)
Fragrant sumac (*Rhus aromatica*)
Memorial rose (*Rosa Wichuraiana*)
Streamco purple osier willow (*Salix purpurea* 'Streamco')
Bumald spirea (*Spiraea* × *Bumalda*)
Crispa cutleaf stephandra (*Stephanandra incisa* 'Crispa')
Chenault coralberry (*Symphoricarpos* × *Chenaultii*)

SHRUBS THAT TOLERATE EXPOSED SITES

The blustery top of a hill or a wind-blown yard beside an open meadow or lake can be difficult sites for most plants. Cold blasts can blow down trees, break the stems of flowers, and cause winter burn on evergreens. To make your open site more amenable to other plants, start by planting a wind break, using durable shrubs that are thoroughly hardy in your area. Evergreens (marked with a asterisk) will cut the wind year-round while deciduous shrubs work best while the leaves are out.

Five-leaf aralia (*Acanthopanax Sieboldianus*)
Chokeberries (*Aronia* spp.)
Japanese barberry (*Berberis Thunbergii*)
Common sweetshrub (*Calycanthus floridus*)
Tartarian dogwood (*Cornus alba*)
Red-osier dogwood (*Cornus sericea*)
Smokebush (*Cotinus Coggygria*)
Spreading cotoneaster (*Cotoneaster divaricatus*)
Hedge cotoneaster (*Cotoneaster lucidus*)
Winged euonymus (*Euonymus alata*)
Sea buckthorn (*Hippophae rhamnoides*)
Panicle hydrangea (*Hydrangea paniculata* 'Grandiflora')
*Chinese juniper (*Juniperus chinensis*)
*Rocky Mountain juniper (*Juniperus scopulorum*)
*Eastern red cedar (*Juniperus virginiana*)
Sweet mock orange (*Philadelphus coronarius*)
Vanhoutten spirea (*Spiraea* × *vanhouttii*)
Thunberg spirea (*Spiraea Thunbergii*)
* Eastern arborvitae, compact forms (*Thuja occidentalis* 'Boothii',
    'Emerald', and others)

BOXWOODS FOR BITTER CHICAGO WINTERS

Boxwood (*Buxus* spp.) has been shunned as an evergreen in very cold winter climates because it is easily damaged by low temperatures. But this is changing. New cultivars of box-wood, brought together by a consortium of the Chicago Botanic Garden, The Morton Arboretum, and the Ornamental Growers Association of Northern Illinois, have been select-ed for their winter hardiness. These selected varieties were grown in an open field, with record winter lows down to -27 degrees F. Those cultivars that survived made the recommended list.

'Glencoe'
'Green Gem'
'Green Mound'
'Green Mountain'
'Green Velvet'
'Fiorii'
'Winter Beauty'

DIANE HEILENMAN'S SHRUBS FOR THE LOWER MIDWEST

The lower Midwest, particularly warmer zone 6 in southern Indiana and Ohio, Kentucky, and Missouri are Heilenman's stomping grounds. A columnist for the Louisville, Kentucky *Courier Journal* and author of *Gardening in the Lower Midwest* (1994; Indiana University Press), she has experimented widely with shrubs and found the following to be exceptional.

Glossy abelia (*Abelia × grandiflora*)
Bottlebrush buckeye (*Aesculus parviflora*)
Bluebeard (*Caryopteris* spp.)
Sweet pepperbush (*Clethra alnifolia*)
Red veined enkianthus (*Enkianthus campanulatus*)
Fothergilla (*Fothergilla* spp.)
Diana rose of Sharon (*Hibiscus syriacus* 'Diana')
Oakleaf hydrangea (*Hydrangea quercifolia*)
Winterberry (*Ilex verticillata*)
Sweetspire (*Itea virginica*)
Mountain laurel (*Kalmia latifolia*)
Brownii honeysuckle (*Lonicera Brownii*)
Staghorn sumac (*Rhus typhina*)
Bridalwreath spirea (*Spiraea vanhouttii*)
Double file viburnum (*Viburnum plicatum*)

"Once upon a time I harbored hopes of growing every plant in existence, a sure sign of a youthful personality weak on the design side. I am older now and reconciled to the sad truth that I cannot. I am simply outnumbered."
Diane Heileman, from Gardening in the Lower Midwest, *1994, Indiana University Press, Bloomington, Indiana*

MEGAN WOLFE'S FAVORITE FLOWERING SHRUBS

Great performance and availability top the list of important criteria for Megan Wolfe, landscape designer from Miller's Beach, Indiana, and landscape consultant for the city of Gary, Indiana. Here are her favorites.

Oak leaf hydrangea (*Hydrangea quercifolia*); has winter presence, rich fall color, and long-lasting flowers
Nikko Blue Hydrangea (*Hydrangea macrophylla* 'Nikko Blue'); true blue flowers, hardy in protected areas of zone 5
PJM rhododendron (*Rhododendron* 'PJM'); good evergreen to use with broad leaf hostas and dark yews
Rugosa roses (*Rosa rugosa*); they can take just about anything
Gold Flame spirea (*Spiraea × Bumalda* 'Gold Flame'); allow single specimens to spread to eight feet across for great architectural presence; bright colors good with evergreens
Bridal wreath spirea (*Spiraea prunifolia*); old-fashioned with reliable white flowers
Miss Kim lilac (*Syringa patula* 'Miss Kim'); stays compact and grows well

American cranberry bush viburnum (*Viburnum trilobum*); white flowers, fall colors, berries for birds, predictable growth

THE FOLLOWING ARE HEARTBREAKERS BUT WORTH TRYING
These shrubs may need extra attention to survive harsh Midwestern winters and other adverse conditions, but because of their great beauty, they are well worth the extra effort.

Japanese beautyberry (*Callicarpa japonica*); needs winter protection; lavender berries against gold and pink fall foliage
Japanese andromeda (*Pieris japonica*); handsome flowers and foliage but deer find it fast

"If you want to know that what you plant is going to work, then you'll stick to tried-and-true favorites like these. Our winters (in northwest Indiana) are supposed to be Zone 5, but we have freak cold snaps that fall well below what they should. It's important to plan ahead for that when deciding on which shrubs to plant."
Megan Wolfe, APLD Certified Landscape Designer, Millers Beach, northwest Indiana

Shrubs through the Seasons

To me, nothing announces spring more vividly than the flowering of Korean spice viburnum (*Viburnum Carlesii*), which blossoms in earliest May and perfumes much of the yard with a wonderful aroma. My favorite for summer is butterfly bush (*Buddleia Davidii*) with sweeping spires of the most intense purple, occasional drafts of perfume, and butterflies galore, which are drawn to the abundant flowers. In autumn, I'm drawn to the tried-and-true burning bush (*Euonymus alata*), perhaps overly common but always beautiful when ablaze with its crimson autumnal leaves. Planning for interest throughout the seasons keeps the landscape lively.

SHRUBS THAT BLOOM FOUR WEEKS OR LONGER

Many classic flowering shrubs, including lilacs, provide intense but short-lived flowers for several weeks each year. The following shrubs can put on an extended show, especially if you remove the fading blossoms to encourage rebloom.

Glossy abelia (*Abelia × grandiflora*)
Butterfly bush (*Buddleia Davidii*)
Summer-sweet (*Clethra alnifolia*)
Rose of Sharon (*Hibiscus syriacus*)
Annabelle hydrangea (*Hydrangea arborescens* 'Annabelle')
Peegee hydrangea (*Hydrangea paniculata* 'Grandiflora')
Oakleaf hydrangea (*Hydrangea quercifolia*)
Mock orange (*Philadelphus coronarius*)
Japanese spirea (*Spiraea japonica*)
Weigela (*Weigela florida*)

A SAMPLER OF SHRUBS FOR FLOWER IN SPRING AND SUMMER

Flowering shrubs are a perfect accompaniment for flowering trees, perennials, or annuals. You will never have to dispair for lack of flowers when you plant from this list of seasonal bloomers.

(You'll notice the conspicuous absence of rhododendrons, azaleas, mountain laurels, and Japanese andromedas. These shrubs need acidic, moist, and well-drained soil and can be difficult to grow; they have been excluded here.)

Common Pearlbush

SPRING-BLOOMING SHRUBS

White forsythia (*Abeliophyllum distichum*)	White
Fragrant winter hazel (*Corylopsis glabrescens*)	Yellow
Rose daphne (*Daphne Cneorum*)	Pink
Slender deutzia (*Deutzia gracilis*)	White
Common pearlbush (*Exochorda racemosa*)	White
Meadowlark forsythia (*Forsythia × intermedia* 'Meadowlark')	Yellow
Fothergillas (*Fothergilla* spp.)	White
Chinese witch hazel (*Hamamelis mollis*)	Yellow
Virginia sweetspire (*Itea virginica*)	White
Japanese kerria (*Kerria japonica*)	Yellow
Oregon grape holly (*Mahonia Aquifolium*)	Yellow
Mock orange (*Philadelphus coronarius*)	White
Baby's breath or Thunberg spirea (*Spiraea Thunbergii*)	White
Bridalwreath spirea (*Spiraea prunifolia*)	White
Lilacs (*Syringa* spp.)	White, lavender, purple, blue
Viburnums (*Viburnum* spp.)	White, pink
Weigela (*Weigela florida*)	Pink, red, white, blue

SUMMER-BLOOMING SHRUBS

Glossy abelia (*Abelia × grandiflora*)	White, pink
Bottlebrush buckeye (*Aesculus parviflora*)	White
Butterfly bush (*Buddleia Davidii*)	White, purple, pink
Summer-sweet (*Clethra alnifolia*)	White
Cinnamon clethra (*Clethra acuminata*)	White
Smokebush (*Cotinus Coggygria*)	Purple
Rose of Sharon (*Hibiscus syriacus*)	Pink, white, purple, blue
Oakleaf hydrangea (*Hydrangea quercifolia*)	White
Panicled hydrangea (*Hydrangea paniculata*)	White
Shrubby St. John's wort (*Hypericum prolificum*)	Yellow

Bush cinquefoil (*Potentilla fruticosa*)	Yellow, red, white, pink
Bumalda spirea (*Spriaea* × *Bumalda*)	White, pink, red
Japanese spirea (*Spiraea japonica*)	White, pink, red

FALL-BLOOMING SHRUBS

Butterfly bush (*Buddleia Davidii*)	White, purple, pink
Witch hazel (*Hamamelis virginiana*)	Yellow
Tardiva panicled hydrangea (*Hydrangea paniculata* 'Tardiva')	White
Rose of Sharon (*Hibiscus syriacus*)	Pink, white purple, blue
Japanese spirea (*Spiraea japonica* 'Shirbori')	White, pink, rose

SPRING BLOOM WITH EXTRA DURABLE RHODODENDRONS

Rhododendrons, which combine the advantages of evergreen foliage, outstanding spring flowers, and preference for light shade, can be finicky to grow. The soil must be rich, moist but well drained, and highly acid. In the Chicago area, where the soil is not particularly promising—being stiff, alkaline clay—small-leaved rhododendrons survive, even thrive; Richard Hawke, plant evaluator for the Chicago Botanic Garden, conducted a five-year trial of small-leaved rhododendrons that are similar or related to stalwart 'PJM' and found the following five cultivars to be the best.

> Milestone rhododendron (*Rhododendron* × 'Milestone')
> Weston's Pink Diamond rhododendron (*Rhododendron* ×
>   'Weston's Pink Diamond')
> Molly Fordham rhododendron (*Rhododendron* × 'Molly Fordham')
> Laurie rhododendron (*Rhododendron* × 'Laurie')
> Pink Clusters rhododendron (*Rhododendron* 'Pink Clusters')

"The evergreen habit, reliable spring bloom, and overall hardiness of 'PJM' [rhododendron] are characteristics sought by gardeners in this harsh climate [Chicago], and its success in the local landscape is due to its adaptability to adverse sites and its ability to thrive in full sun. Its bright lavender-pink flowers are a welcome sight after a long Midwestern winter. No other rhododendron fills the local landscape niche for broad-leaved evergreens better than 'PJM'."

Richard Hawke, Coordinator of Plant Evaluation Programs, Chicago Botanic Garden, *from* **Plant Evaluation Notes**, *Volume 1, No. 1*

WITCH HAZELS FOR OFF-SEASON FLOWERS

Witch hazels, which double as large shrubs or small trees, produce spiderlike flowers in the autumn after the leaves have fallen or early in spring before the leaves open —the timing varying with the species. Charmed by the off-season flowers and the handsome multiple trunks and interesting toothed leaves, I think witch hazels deserve their own list. The Missouri Botanical Garden has been collecting witch hazels for forty years, and Chip Tynan, horticulturist and garden information specialist, was drafted to share his favorites.

Arnold Promise witch hazel (*Hamamelis* × *intermedia* 'Arnold Promise')
Copper Beauty witch hazel (*Hamamelis* × *intermedia* 'Copper Beauty')
Jelena witch hazel (*Hamamelis* × *intermedia* 'Jelena')
Chinese witch hazel (*Hamamelis mollis*)
Pallida Chinese witch hazel (*Hamamelis mollis* 'Pallida')
Ozark or vernal witch hazel (*Hamamelis vernalis*)
Common witch hazel (*Hamamelis virginiana*)

"Witch hazels are great plants, my favorite being the fragrant flowered ones—*Hamamelis virginiana* and *H. vernalis*. It takes a while before they grow to a good size, but the bigger they are, the more spectacular they are. Some of the oldest on Missouri Botanical Garden grounds have developed intriguing branching patterns with limbs that arch to the ground and come back up again. That's a memorable plant!"
Chip Tynan, Missouri Botanical Garden horticulturist

DECIDUOUS SHRUBS FOR GOOD FALL COLOR

Shade trees are not the only deciduous plants to revel in the end of the growing season. Shrubs such as burning bush (winged euonymus; *euonymus alata*), sumac (*Rhus* spp.), and fothergilla are famous for their blazing fall leaf color. Beyond these well-known autumn celebrities are many others that will add to the jubilee.

Chokecherry (*Aronia* spp. especially A. *arbutifolia* 'Brilliantissima')	Red
Barberries (*Berberis* spp.)	Red
Beautybush (*Kolkwitzia amabilis*)	Yellow
Common sweetshrub (*Calycanthus floridus*)	Yellow
Summer-sweet clethra (*Clethra alnifolia*)	Yellow
Smokebush (*Cotinus Coggygria*)	Yellow to red
Cranberry cotoneaster (*Cotoneaster apiculata*)	Red
Spreading cotoneaster (*Cotoneaster divaricatus*)	Yellow, purple, or red
Red veined enkianthus (*Enkianthus campanulatus*)	Red
Burning bush (*Euonymus alata*)	Red
Fothergilla (*Fothergilla* spp.)	Red
Witch hazel (*Hamamelis* spp.)	Yellow
Oakleaf hydrangea (*Hydrangea quercifolia*)	Red
Virginia sweetspire (*Itea virginica*)	Red
Smooth sumac (*Rhus glabra*)	Red, yellow, or orange

Fragrant sumac (*Rhus aromatica*)	Red, yellow or orange
Flaming Globe spirea (*Spiraea* × 'Flaming Globe')	
Arrowwood viburnum (*Viburnum dentatum*)	Red
Linden viburnum (*Viburnum dilatatum*)	Burgundy
Double file viburnum (*Viburnum plicatum* var. *tomentosum*)	Burgundy

EVERGREEN SHRUBS WITH HANDSOME WINTER FOLIAGE

For winter cheer, every yard needs a dose of evergreens. Don't be fooled, however, by the promise of spring greenery in midwinter because some evergreens turn shades of red, gold, bronze, or burgundy in fall and remain that way until spring. 'Aglo' rhododendron, a smaller leaf hybrid well-liked by Cleveland-area designer Alexander Apanius, turns red in fall and winter. Creeping mahonia turns an attractive purple in winter.

You may find that broad-leaf evergreens, so lush during the warmer seasons, may struggle in cold, blustery winter weather. The foliage of leatherleaf viburnums and large-leaved rhododendrons will curl up and lose some of their attractiveness. Water broad-leaf evergreens well into the autumn and early winter and apply an antidessicants to limit water loss through the leaves and minimize winter problems.

BROAD-LEAVED ERICACEOUS EVERGREEN SHRUBS

The Ericaceae family of shrubs are well-known for winter interest. It bears repeating that these plants need special conditions—acid soil that's moist but well drained and amended with plenty of organic material.

> Meserve hybrid hollies (*Ilex* × *Meserveae* 'Blue Girl', 'Blue Princess', 'China Boy', and others)
> Japanese holly (*Ilex crenata*)
> Mountain laurel (*Kalmia latifolia*)
> Drooping leucothoe (*Leucothoe Fontanesiana*)
> Oregon grape holly (*Mahonia Aquifolium*)
> Japanese andromeda (*Pieris japonica*)
> Rhododendrons (*Rhododendron* spp.)

BROAD-LEAVED NONERICACEOUS EVERGREEN SHRUBS

These evergreens do not insist on special acidic soils and can be easier to grow in much of the Midwest.

> Wintergreen littleleaf boxwood (*Buxus microphylla* 'Wintergreen')
> Dwarf hinoki false cypress (*Chamaecyparis obtusa* 'Nana')
> Thread leaf Japanese false cypress (*Chamaecyparis pisifera* 'Filifera')
> Bearberry cotoneaster (*Cotoneaster Dammeri*)
> Wintercreeper euonymus (*Euonymus Fortunei* 'Sun Spot', 'Emerald 'n Gold', and other shrubby cultivars)
> Junipers (*Juniperus* spp.)
> Yews (*Taxus* spp.)
> Arborvitae (*Thuja* spp.)

SHRUBS WITH BERRIES FOR WINTER INTEREST

Berries, like precious jewels, sparkle on some shrubs in summer, fall, and even winter. You can build a color scheme around the most prominent by matching the red of cotoneasters (*Cotoneaster* spp.) to crimson mums or the blue of Oregon grape holly (*Mahonia Aquifolium*) to blue or violet pansies. I am always particularly impressed by the sprays of red rose hips on the multiflora rose, which can be used to make an awesome autumn wreath. Shrubs marked with an asterisk ordinarily hold their berries into the winter. Berries that disappear earlier often are eaten by birds, who bring their own fleeting beauty into the yard.

RED OR ORANGE BERRIES
*Red chokeberry (*Aronia arbutifolia*)
*Korean barberry (*Berberis koreana*)
*Japanese barberry (*Berberis Thunbergii*)
Cranberry cotoneaster (*Cotoneaster apiculata*)
Creeping cotoneaster (*Cotoneaster adpressus*)
Many-flowered cotoneaster (*Cotoneaster multiflorus*)
*Autumn olive (*Elaeagnus umbellata*)
Common winterberry (*Ilex verticillata*)
Meserve hybrid hollies (*Ilex* × *Meserveae*)
*Morrow honeysuckle (*Lonicera Morrowii*)
Oriental photinia (*Photinia villosa*)
*Chadwick scarlet fire thorn (*Pyracantha coccinea* 'Chadwickii')
Chenault coralberry (*Symphoricarpos* × *Chenaultii* 'Hancock')
*Canadian, Japanese, and Anglojap yew
   (*Taxus canadensis*, *T. cuspidata*, and *T.* × *media*)
*European cranberry bush viburnum (*Viburnum Opulus*)
Sergeant viburnum (*Viburnum Sargentii*)
*American cranberry bush viburnum (*Viburnum trilobum*)
Viburnums (*Viburnum* spp.)

European
Cranberry Bush
Viburnum

BLACK, PURPLE, OR BLUE BERRIES
Black and purple chokeberry (*Aronia melanocarpa*; *A. prunifolia*)
Japanese beautyberry (*Callicarpa japonica*)
*Junipers (*Juniperus* spp.)
*Inkberry holly (*Ilex glabra*)
*Oregon grape holly (*Mahonia Aquifolium*)

WHITE AND GRAY BERRIES
Common snowberry (*Symphoricarpos albus*)
Tartarian dogwood (*Cornus alba*)
Red-osier dogwood (*Cornus sericea*)
Gray dogwood (*Cornus racemosa*)
*Bayberry (*Myrica pensylvanica*)

Shrubs in the Landscape

Shrubs are to a landscape what furniture is to a living room—a functional and decorative necessity. They can be plump and cushy, very relaxing to be around. Or they can be firm and formal, giving a precise look that encourages one to sit up straight. Shrubs for varying landscape uses follow.

SHRUBS WITH PURPLE, GOLD, OR VARIEGATED FOLIAGE

Flowers aren't the only way to brighten up a landscape. Consider adding a few shrubs with unique foliage colors. Some of the most popular of these are notoriously overused, but unless you are trying to awe the neighborhood horticultural crowd, they can still do a good job in your yard.

RED OR PURPLE LEAVES
Purple leaf barberry (*Berberis Thunbergii* 'Atropurpurea' and other cultivars)
Gouchaultii Tartarian dogwood (*Cornus alba* 'Gouchaultii')
Velvet cloak smokebush (*Cotinus Coggygria* 'Velvet Cloak')
Girard's Rainbow leucothoe (*Leucothoe Fontanesiana* 'Girard's Rainbow')
Purpleleaf sand cherry (*Prunus* × *cistena*)
Onondaga sergent viburnum (*Viburnum Sargentii* 'Onondaga')

GOLDEN LEAVES
Golden barberry (*Berberis Thunbergii* 'Aurea' and other cultivars)
Golden Hinoki false cypress (*Chamaecyparis obtusa* 'Aurea' and other cultivars)
Golden Japanese false cypress (*Chamaecyparis pisifera* 'Filifera')
Spaethii Tartarian dogwood (*Cornus alba* 'Spaethii')
Golden Chinese junipers (*Juniperus chinensis* 'Gold Coast', 'Saybrook Gold', and other cultivars)
Golden creeping junipers (*Juniperus horizontalis* 'Mother Lode' and other cultivars)
Bumald's spirea/Japanese spirea (*Spiraea* × *Bumalda*; *S. japonica* 'Gold Mound', 'Golden Carpet', 'Golden Globe', and other cultivars)
Arborvitae (*Thuja occidentalis* 'Aurea', 'Rheingold', and other cultivars)

VARIEGATED FOLIAGE
Variegated Tartarian dogwood (*Cornus alba* 'Argenteo-marginata')
Variegated blood-twig dogwood (*Cornus sanguinea* 'Variegata')
Variegated red-osier dogwood (*Cornus sericea* 'Silver and Gold' and 'Sunshine')
Variegated wintercreeper (*Euonymus Fortunei* 'Sun Spot', and other cultivars)
Variegated mock orange (*Philadelphus coronarius* 'Variegatus')
Variegated Weigela (*Weigela florida* 'Variegata')

TIM CHRISTIE'S FAVORITE SHRUBS FOR MATURE LANDSCAPES

If you have recently purchased an older home with a once-elegant landscape, there is much you can do to bring it back to life. Tim Christie, former president of the Association of Professional Landscape Designers, Chicago-area landscape designer, specializes in just such landscape restorations. He recommends using the following shade-tolerant shrubs that have a special elegance.

Serviceberries, multitrunked (*Amelanchier* spp.)
Glencoe boxwood (*Buxus* × 'Glencoe')
Summer-sweet (*Clethra alnifolia*)
Witch hazel (*Hamamelis* spp.)
Ward's yew (*Taxus* × *media* 'Wardii')
Judd viburnum (*Viburnum* × *Juddii*)
Leatherleaf viburnum (*Viburnum rhytidophyllum*)

UPDATING AN OLDER LANDSCAPE

"Most often when a landscape is renovated it changes somewhat to reflect the current time and conditions. The bones of the mature landscape, the trees and shrubs, may have changed the landscape character from sunny to shady as they have grown over the years.

"Consider how you can save the mature trees and shrubs and bring them back to good working order. Then think about what plants have become available since the house and yard were originally planned and could add extra interest, working well among existing plants.

"Finally, consider your own objectives, which might be different than the original owners. Many people today are getting away from standard foundation plantings and may want privacy, welcoming front entrances, or other elements. All these ideas come together when formulating a new garden plan."

Tim Christie, former president of the Association of Professional Landscape Designers (APLD) and Certified Landscape Designer from Chicago

SHRUBS THAT ATTRACT HUMMINGBIRDS AND BUTTERFLIES

Nature lovers delight in a fluttering butterfly or hummingbird pausing to drink the nectar of shrubby flowers.

BUTTERFLY-ATTRACTING SHRUBS

Butterfly bush (*Buddleia* hybrids)
Cotoneaster (*Cotoneaster* spp.)
Russian olive (*Elaeagnus angustifolia*)
Rose of Sharon (*Hibiscus syriacus*)
Honeysuckle (*Lonicera* spp.)
Rhododendrons (*Rhododendron* spp.)
Weigela (*Weigela* spp.)

HUMMINGBIRD-ATTRACTING SHRUBS

Azaleas (*Rhododendron* spp.)
Butterfly bush (*Buddleia Davidii*)
Cotoneaster (*Cotoneaster* spp.)
Russian olive (*Elaeagnus angustifolia*)
Rose of Sharon (*Hibiscus syriacus*)
Beautybush (*Kolkwitzia amabilis*)
Honeysuckle (*Lonicera* spp.)
Rhododendron (*Rhododendron* spp.)
Weigela (*Weigela florida*)

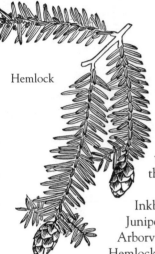

Hemlock

EVERGREEN SHRUBS FOR A CLIPPED HEDGE

A clipped hedge, although maintenance intensive, can do wonderful things in a landscape. It makes a marvelous backdrop for a flower garden, creates privacy, and muffles loud noises. Make sure to clip the top of the hedge narrower than the bottom so the sides taper outward and receive plenty of sun. The following plants are well-suited for both formal and low-maintenance, informal hedges that are never sheared.

Inkberry holly (*Ilex glabra*)
Juniper (*Juniperus* spp.)
Arborvitaes (*Thuja* spp.)
Hemlock (*Tsuga canadensis*)
Yews (*Taxus* spp.)

ALEX APANIUS'S FAVORITE COMPACT EVERGREENS

When using evergreens around the house, choose cultivars and species that are naturally low growing and won't require any pruning for height control. There are more choices of these easy-care evergreens than ever before. The following are some of the favorites of Alexander Apanius, landscape designer in Greater Cleveland and former executive director of The Garden Center of Greater Cleveland (now the Cleveland Botanical Garden).

Kingsville dwarf boxwood (*Buxus microphylla* 'Kingsville Dwarf')
Dwarf hinoki false cypress (*Chamaecyparis obtusa* 'Nana')
Aglo rhododendron (*Rhododendron* × 'Aglo')
American-Japanese hybrid everlow yew (*Taxus* × *media* 'Everlow')
Compact Canadian hemlock (*Tsuga canadensis* 'Compacta')
Sergent Chinese juniper (*Juniperus chinensis* var. *Sargentii*)

SHRUBS WITH BOLD, COARSE-TEXTURED FOLIAGE

Shrubs with big, bold leaves make interesting contrasts when blended with shrubs with smaller or finer leaves (like spireas and hypericums) or when showcased amid flowers and herbs.

Oakleaf hydrangea (*Hydrangea quercifolia*)
Peegee hydrangea (*Hydrangea paniculata* 'Grandiflora')
Rhododendrons, large-leaf types (*Rhododendron* spp.)
Oregon grape holly (*Mahonia Aquifolium*)
Leatherleaf viburnum (*Viburnum rhytidophyllum*)

SHRUBS WITH FRAGRANT BLOSSOMS

A few elite shrubs have both perfume and great flowers. These combined virtues make them particularly nice to use near an open window or along a walk where you'll enjoy them often.

Sweet shrub (*Calycanthus floridus*)
Fragrant winter hazel (*Corylopsis glabrescens*)
Rose daphne (*Daphne Cneorum*)
Fothergillas (*Fothergilla* spp.)
Winter honeysuckle (*Lonicera fragrantissima*)
Mock orange (*Philadelphus coronarius*)
Lilacs (*Syringa* spp.)
Burkwood viburnum (*Viburnum × Burkwoodii*)
Korean spice viburnum (*Viburnum Carlessii*)
Fragrant snowball (*Viburnum × carlcephalum*)
Judd's viburnum (*Viburnum × Juddii*)

SHRUBS THAT MAKE GOOD GROUND COVERS

Instead of growing upward, some shrubs grow outward. These creeping shrubs make a carpet of foliage, sometimes rooting as they spread, and often extending many feet from the original planting. Because their lifeline is a woody stem, few can tolerate being trod on much, so they are best limited to garden beds or banks. Those marked with an asterisk are evergreen.

Prostrate abelia (*Abelia × grandiflora* 'Prostrata')
*Bearberry cotoneaster (*Cotoneaster Dammeri*)
Rockspray cotoneaster (*Cotoneaster horizontalis*)
*Creeping junipers (*Juniperus chinensis, J. conferta, J. horizontalis*)
*Oregon grape holly (*Mahonia Aquifolium*)
*Russian arborvitae (*Thuja* spp.))
*Creeping yew (*Taxus × media* 'Everlow')

SHRUBS THAT CAN DOUBLE AS MULTI-TRUNKED TREES

Some large shrubs can also be used as trees if you remove the lower limbs to display the main branches as trunks. And some small trees can be purchased in a multi-trunk form to be used as large shrubs.

> Serviceberries (*Amelanchier* spp.)
> Cornelian cherry dogwood (*Cornus mas*)
> Star magnolia (*Magnolia stellata*)
> Lilac (*Syringa vulgaris*)
> Staghorn sumac (*Rhus typhina*)
> Witch hazels (*Hamamelis* spp.)

NARROW, UPRIGHT SHRUBS FOR TIGHT PLACES

Slender upright shrubs, with a proper posture that would make mothers envious, fit easily into small spaces and offer an emphatic contrast to low-growing or mounded shrubs. Blending several into a garden, perhaps framing a doorway or the entrance to the walk, provides a more formal flavor. Those marked with an asterisk are evergreen.

> Titan autumn olive (*Elaegnus angustifolia* 'Tizam')
> Red-vein enkianthus (*Enkianthus campanulatus*)
> *Chinese juniper (*Juniperus chinensis* 'Columnaris', 'Mountbatten', 'Hooks',
>   'Obelisk', and others)
> *Common juniper (*Juniperus communis* 'Sentinel' and others)
> * Rocky Mountain juniper (*Juniperus scopulorum* 'Skyrocket', 'Gray Gleam',
>   'Medora' and others)
> *Dwarf Alberta spruce (*Picea glauca* 'Conica')
> Columnar glossy buckthorn (*Rhamnus Frangula* 'Columnaris')
> Japanese-American yew (*Taxus* × *media* 'Hicksii', 'Old Westbury', and others)
> *Eastern arborvitae (*Thuja occidentalis* 'Emerald', 'Wintergreen', and others)

PERENNIALS AND ORNAMENTAL GRASSES

If there is an ideal kind of plant for the Midwest, perennials fill the bill. Plants that live for several to many years, perennials are a mixed lot united primarily by their ability to be sheltered underground in winter. Where the earth is heavy and sodden, building a raised bed that drains well will provide a healthy subterranean environment.

Perennials, of which there are thousands, have many and varying qualities that make them marvelous to mix into creative combinations. There are more perennials than most people can grow, or even know, and perennial elitists will try to impress you with their encyclopedic knowledge. Don't let this discourage you. Find perennials that you like and that will perform well in your yard and gradually expand your plant palette.

Most perennials bloom only for a portion of the growing season. Christmas roses (*Helleborus* spp.) flower with the earliest dawning of spring, while irises (*Iris* spp.) and peonies (*Paeonia* spp.) peak as spring weather becomes warm. Later, coneflowers (*Echinacea* spp.) and coreopsis (*Coreopsis* spp.) take over for a long, luxurious stretch in summer and early fall. In autumn, asters (*Aster* spp.) and chrysanthemums (*Chrysanthemum* spp.) finish the gardening year with panache. Obviously, bloom time becomes an important consideration when planning a garden. In an all-purpose garden, you may want to plan for perennials that will provide interest throughout the seasons. But where one all-out assault on the senses is needed at a critical time, cluster simultaneous bloomers for spectacular results.

Right Plant, Right Place

Because most gardens have a few growing kinks (mine has infertile clay left when a worn-out farm field was recycled into a homesite), it's good to know which perennials are predisposed to generously ignoring them. Once you know the limiting factors of your yard, consult the following lists to choose the perennials that will work best for you.

PERENNIALS FOR ALKALINE SOIL

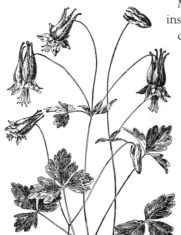

Many parts of the Midwest—around Chicago and Cincinnati, for instance—have limestone-based soil with a high pH. It is rich in calcium and not as fertile as slightly acidic soils. If your soil is slightly alkaline, easily identified by a pH or soil test, avoid rhododendrons and their kin and plant perennials that thrive in sweet soils. Where soils are highly alkaline, even the following may fail. Ask your Cooperative Extension Agent how to bring the soil back into a more reliable pH range.

Wild columbine (*Aquilegia canadensis*)
Rockcress (*Aubrieta deltoidea*)
Bergenia (*Bergenia cordifolia*)
Red valerian (*Centranthus ruber*)
Leadwort (*Ceratostigma plumbaginoides*)
Chrysanthemums (*Dendranthema* spp.; syn. *Chrysantemum* spp.)
Lanceleaf coreopsis (*Coreopsis lanceolata*)
Pinks (*Dianthus* spp.)

Wild
Columbine

Bleeding-hearts (*Dicentra* spp.)
Gas plant (*Dictamnus albus*)
Purple coneflower (*Echinacea purpurea*)
Globe thistle (*Echinops Ritro*)
Ravenna grass (*Erianthus ravennae*)
Hardy geraniums (*Geranium* spp.)
Baby's breath (*Gypsophila* spp.)
Candytuft (*Iberis sempervirens*)
English lavender (*Lavandula angustifolia*)
Shasta daisy (*Leucanthemum × superbum*; syn. *Chrysanthemum × superbum*)
German catchfly (*Lychnis Viscaria*)
Maiden grasses (*Miscanthus* spp.)
Fountain grasses (*Pennisetum* spp.)
Pincushion flower (*Scabiosa caucasica*)
Little bluestem (*Schizachyrium scoparium*)

GREG SPEICHERT'S PERENNIALS FOR WATER GARDENS

Water gardens double your enjoyment of perennials. You get to see both the flowers and their rippling images in a mirrorlike pool. A delightful and unique array of plants are suited to water gardens. Water garden plants are divided roughly into two classes: *aquatics*, or water plants that must be partly or mostly submerged in water most of the time, and *marginals*, or bog plants, that do best along the wet or marshy margins of a pond or water garden. There's nobody better to share a list than Greg Speichert, plant collector and owner of Crystal Palace Perennials, a water garden nursery in Cedar Lake, Indiana.

AQUATIC WATER PLANTS

Water willow (*Justicia americana*)
Lotus (*Nelumbo* spp. including pink to yellow 'Carolina Queen'; vari-

colored 'Mrs. Perry D. Slocum' and 'Perry's Super Star'; and pink 'China Pink Cup')

Water lilies (*Nymphaea* spp. including pink 'Yuh Ling'; red 'Perry's Red Baby'; red and white 'Wucai'; pink to white 'Walter Pagels'; yellow 'Joey Tomocik'; yellow and pink 'Florida Sunset'; and dark red 'Almost Black')

reeds (*Phragmites* spp. Candy Stripe and Gold Rush Reed)

Frogfruit (*Phyla lanceolata*)

Crown Point pickerel plant (*Pontederia cordata* 'Crown Point')

Bloomin' Baby arrowhead (*Sagittaria* spp. 'Bloomin' Baby')

Zebra rush (*Juncus Tabernaemontana*)

American brooklime (*Veronica americana*)

BOG PLANTS

Marsh marigold (*Caltha palustris*)

Marvell's Gold iris (*Iris fulva* 'Marvell's Gold')

Gem Dandy iris (*Iris* × *robusta* 'Gem Dandy')

Mysterious Monique blue flag (*Iris versicolor* 'Mysterious Monique')

Purple Fan southern blue flag (*Iris virginica* 'Purple Fan')

Ragged robin (*Lychnis Flos-cuculi*)

Butterbur (*Petasites hybridus*)

Marsh
Marigold

"Bog plants can vary in the amount of moisture they require, be it saturated or just constantly damp. They share the trait of not doing well in water over their crown."
Greg Speichert, Crystal Palace Perennials, Cedar Lake, Indiana

PERENNIALS FOR SUN AND WELL-DRAINED SOIL

In contrast to the plants listed in the previous section, the following perennials insist on sharp drainage and lean soil, usually with a high percentage of sand. Every silver-leaved plant and most succulents that I can think of fit in this category. Where soils are less than light, these perennials may grow best in the screen behind a retaining wall, beside a stone walk, or in a container garden where the soil is customized to their requirements.

Yarrow (*Achillea* spp.)

Golden marguerite (*Anthemis tinctoria*)

Sea thrift (*Armeria maritima*)

Artemisia (*Artemisia* spp.)

Maiden pinks (*Dianthus deltoides*)

Sea holly (*Eryngium amethystinum*)

Blanket flower (*Gaillardia* spp.)

English lavender (*Lavandula angustifolia*)

Russian sage (*Perovskia atriplicifolia*)

Lavender cotton (*Santolina Chamaecyparissus*)

Stonecrop (*Sedum* spp.)

Hen and chickens (*Sempervivum tectorum*)

Lamb's ear (*Stachys byzantina*)

Rose verbena (*Verbena canadensis*)

PERENNIALS FOR HEAVY CLAY SOIL

Clay soil is the norm around the Midwest. Composed of tightly packed, minute mineral particles, clay tends to stay cold and wet late into spring, then harden into brick if allowed to dry out during summer. Add as much compost as you can get your hands on—ordering a truckload from a municipal composting project is not overkill. The following perennials will thrive in the now-amended mix.

Bugleweed (*Ajuga* spp.)
Lady's mantle (*Alchemilla mollis*)
Willow blue star (*Amsonia Tabernaemontana*)
Snowdrop anemone (*Anemone sylvestris*)
Japanese anemone (*Anemone × hybrida*)
Grape-leaf anemone (*Anemone tomentosa* `Robustissima')
Chinese anemone (*Anemone hupehensis*)
Columbines (*Aquilegia* spp.)
Heath aster (*Aster ericoides*)
Calico aster (*Aster lateriflorus*)
New England aster (*Aster novae-angliae*)
Astilbe (*Astilbe* spp.)
Baptisia (*Baptisia* spp.)
Boltonia (*Boltonia asteroides*)
Carpatican bellflower (*Campanula carpatica*)
Clustered bellflower (*Campanula glomerata*)
Leadwort (*Ceratostigma plumbaginoides*)
Golden star (*Chrysogonum virginianum*)
Black snakeroot (*Cimicifuga racemosa*)
Lily-of-the-valley (*Convallaria majalis*)
Coreopsis (*Coreopsis* spp.)
Foxgloves (*Digitalis* spp.)
Purple coneflower (*Echinacea purpurea*)
Pale coneflower (*Echinacea pallida*)
Trout lily (*Erythronium americanum*)
Joe-Pye weed (*Eupatorium* spp.)
Siberian meadowsweet (*Filipendula palmata*)
Queen-of-the-prairie (*Filipendula rubra*)
Sweet woodruff (*Galium odoratum*)
Hardy geraniums (*Geranium* spp.)
Sneezeweed (*Helenium* spp.)
Perennial sunflower (*Helianthus* spp.)
Sunflower heliopsis (*Heliopsis helianthoides*)
Daylily (*Hemerocallis* spp.)
Coralbells (*Heuchera* spp.)
Hosta (*Hosta* spp.)
Dead nettle (*Lamium maculatum*)
Siberian iris (*Iris sibirica*)
Lobelias (*Lobelia* spp.)
Peony (*Paeonia* spp.)

Oriental poppies (*Papaver orientale*)
Obedient plant (*Physostegia virginiana*)
Balloon flower (*Platycodon grandiflorus*)
Coneflowers (*Rudbeckia* spp.)
Autumn Joy sedum (*Sedum* × 'Autumn Joy')
Goldenrod (*Solidago* spp.)
Spiderwort (*Tradescantia* spp.)

PERENNIALS FOR MOIST SOIL

Moist soils come in two types—damp and spongy or downright drenched. Perennials such as marsh marigolds and ligularia prefer true wetlands—the banks of streams or low marshy areas. (These are identified with an asterisk.) On the less extreme side, woodland wildflowers like Virginia bluebells and Solomon's seal need constant moisture to prevent premature dormancy. Siberian iris must stay moist for at least a season after planting then will tolerate drier soils at times. Daylilies, nature's gift to the gardener, are the only perennial to survive a swampy spring in a low area of my garden, followed by drought just a month or two later.

Astilbes (*Astilbe* spp.)
*Marsh marigold (*Caltha palustris*)
Sedges (*Carex* spp.)
Turtlehead (*Chelone* spp.)
Bleeding hearts (*Dicentra* spp.)
Fairy-bells (*Disporum sessile*)
Leopard's bane (*Doronicum orientale*)
Joe-Pye weed (*Eupatorium* spp.)
Siberian meadowsweet (*Filipendula palmata*)
Queen-of-the-prairie (*Filipendula rubra*)
Common sneezeweed (*Helenium autumnale*)
Daylilies (*Hemerocallis* spp.)
*Houttuynia (*Houttuynia cordata*)
*Yellow flag (*Iris Pseudacorus*)
Siberian iris (*Iris sibirica*)
*Blue flag (*Iris versicolor*)
*Ligularia (*Ligularia* spp.)
Cardinal flower (*Lobelia cardinalis*)
Great blue lobelia (*Lobelia siphilitica*)
Virginia bluebell (*Mertensia virginica*)
Bee balm (*Monarda* spp.)
Forget-me-not (*Myosotis scorpioides*)
Solomon's seal (*Polygonatum* spp.)
Snakeweed (*Polygonum Bistorta*)
*Drumstick primrose (*Primula denticulata*)
*Japanese primrose (*Primula japonica*)
Rodgersia (*Rodgersia* spp.)
False Solomon's seal (*Smilacina racemosa*)
Foam flowers (*Tiarella cordifolia*)

Blue Flag

PERENNIALS THAT TOLERATE SUN OR LIGHT SHADE

The majority of perennials perform best in full sun, ideally six or more hours per day. But in gardens where trees, fences, or walls sometimes block the sun, choose those perennials that will tolerate a little shade. In sunnier locations, they are likely to stay more compact and flower more vigorously but need more watering and mulching to keep them moist. In lightly shaded sites, flowering may not be as profuse, but bright flower colors may stay purer and the blooms may last longer.

Carpet bugleweed (*Ajuga reptans*)
Lady's mantle (*Alchemilla mollis*)
Alkanet (*Anchusa azurea*)
Japanese anemone (*Anemone × hybrida*)
Columbines (*Aquilegia* spp.)
Fall astilbe (*Astilbe Taquetii*)
Bergenia (*Bergenia* spp.)
Bellflower (*Campanula* spp.)
Black snakeroot (*Cimicifuga racemosa*)
Western bleeding heart (*Dicentra formosa*)
Fringed bleeding heart (*Dicentra eximia*)
Foxglove (*Digitalis mertonensis*)
Hardy geraniums (*Geranium* spp.)
Daylilies (*Hemerocallis* spp.)
Coralbells (*Heuchera sanguinea*)
Bee balm (*Monarda didyma*)
Balloon flower (*Platycodon grandiflorus*)
Jacob's ladder (*Polemonium caeruleum*)
Meadow rue (*Thalictrum aquilegifolium*)
Spiderwort (*Tradescantia* spp.)

Balloon Flower

PERENNIALS THAT DO WELL IN SHADE

Where sunlight strikes the springtime earth before a tree's leaves emerge, peeks through foliage in dappled sunlit patches, or slips beneath tall canopies in the morning or evening, these shade-doting flowers will thrive. If planted between tree roots, provide extra fertilizer and water so flowers won't be left parched and starved.

Windflower (*Anemone blanda*)
Astilbe (*Astilbe* spp.)
Chinese forget-me-not (*Brunnera macrophylla*)
Green and gold (*Chrysogonum virginianum*)
Lily-of-the-valley (*Convallaria majalis*)
Dutchman's breeches (*Dicentra Cucullaria*)
Epimedium (*Epimedium* spp.)
Sweet woodruff (*Galium odoratum*)
Christmas/Lenten roses (*Helleborus* spp.)
Hostas (*Hosta* spp.)
Cardinal flower (*Lobelia cardinalis*)

Big blue lobelia (*Lobelia siphilitica*)
Virginia bluebell (*Mertensia virginica*)
Woodland phlox (*Phlox divaricata*)
Solomon's seal (*Polygonatum* spp.)
Cowslips (*Pulmonaria* spp.)
Foamflower (*Tiarella cordifolia*)
Toad lily (*Tricyrtis hirta*)
Violets (*Viola* spp.)

SUSAN BEARD'S EXCEPTIONAL PERENNIALS FOR SHADE

Susan Beard's outstanding shade garden of wildflowers, bulbs, and perennials stretches beside winding paths in the woods behind her Chicago-area home. She shared a list of some of the most outstanding, bright bloomers and foliage plants for light to medium shade.

Catlin's Giant bugleweed (*Ajuga reptans* 'Catlin's Giant')
Purple Sensation flowering onion (*Allium aflatunense* 'Purple Sensation')
Wood garlic (*Allium ursinum*)
Zebdanse flowering onion (*Allium zebdanense*)
Wild ginger (*Asarum canadense*)
European ginger (*Asarum europaeum*)
Chinese forget-me-not (*Brunnera macrophylla*)
Pink turtlehead (*Chelone Lyonii*)
Hardy ageratum (*Eupatorium coelestinum*)
Wild geranium (*Geranium maculatum*)
White bloody cranesbill (*Geranium sanguineum* 'Album')
Christmas rose (*Helleborus niger*)
Lenten rose (*Helleborus orientalis*)
Hostas (*Hosta* spp.)
Forget-me-nots (*Myosotis sylvatica*)
Jacob's ladder (*Polemonium reptans*)
Solomon's seal (*Polygonatum* spp.)
Primrose (*Primula vulgaris*)
Long leaf lungwort (*Pulmonaria longifolia* 'Bertram Anderson'
    and 'Roy Davidson')
False Solomon's seal (*Smilacina racemosa*)
Starry false Solomon's seal (*Smilacina stellata*)
Meadow rue (*Thalictrum aquilegifolium*)

"I like to take plants that are invasive, like bee balm (*Monarda didyma*), golden leaved creeping Jenny (*Lysimachia nummularia* 'Aurea'), and Dame's rocket (*Hesperis matronalis*), and put them in some shade. They often do very well there."
    Susan Beard, plant collector and garden designer for Creative Buyers, Chicago, Illinois

HOSTAS LEAST GNAWED BY SLUGS

Susan Beard's Chicago garden is graced by 250 cultivars of hostas, plus two nosy springer spaniels who make it impossible to set out poisonous baits for slugs. Beard has noticed that hostas with an abundance of tender white on the leaves are often riddled by slugs. When they begin looking shabby, she mows them back and lets them resprout cleanly. Other hostas, including the following, are less troubled by slugs and are good choices for damp areas or organic gardens.

MEDIUM-SMALL
'Pearl Lake'
'Golden Tiara'

MEDIUM SIZED
'Love Pat'

VERY LARGE
H. Sieboldiana 'Elegans'
H. Sieboldiana 'Mira'
'Green Angel'
'Sum and Substance'
'Blue Angel'
'Big Daddy'

VASE SHAPED
'Krossa Regal'
'Regal Splendor'

GOLD LEAVED
'Midas Touch'
'Gold Standard'
'Zounds'
'Little Aurora'

BLUE GREEN AND GOLD OR UNUSUAL VARIEGATION
H. tokudama 'Aureo-nebulosa'
'Color Glory'
'Grand Master'

GORDON OSLUND'S HOSTAS FOR SHADE

Gordon Oslund, grower and partner in Shady Oaks Nursery in Waseca, Minnesota, handles hundreds of different hostas every year and has the unique responsibility of trying out the newest and best for the Midwest. Here are some of his favorite cultivars.

'Emerald Tiara' (green margin and gold center)
'Paul's Glory' (gold heart-shaped leaves with blue-green streaked margin)
'Abiqua Drinking Gourd' (blue-green, round, puckered, cupped leaf)

'Blue Angel' (huge blue leaves, many white flowers)
'Patriot' (dark green centers and wide white margins)
'Regal Splendor' (creamy white leaf margins on frosty blue leaves)
H. *montana* 'Aureomarginata' (large green leaves with irregular margins of yellow turning to cream)
H. *tokudama* 'Flavocircinalis' (broad blue-green leaves with irregular gold margins)

"These popular shade perennials remain attractive from their spring emergence until autumn frost. Handsome foliage grows lush in nearly all soil conditions. Hostas are hardy, long-lived perennials fitting a wide range of shade tolerance and climatic zones (zones 3 to 9). Each year the clump increases in dimension and therefore in value, rewarding the gardener with many years of their beauty, diversity, and durability."
Gordon Oslund, Shady Oaks Nursery

MICHELLE D'ARCY'S ORNAMENTAL GRASSES HARDY IN CHICAGOLAND

Low, tufted grasses, with leaves of interesting shades of green, blue, or red, make a handsome contrast with flowering perennials, shrubs, or evergreens. Taller grasses make marvelous screens and are particularly interesting when ruffling in the breeze. When ornamental grasses, even those supposed to be hardy in Zone 5, melt away during winter, they leave gardeners scratching their heads in puzzlement. To avoid this problem, grow the most reliably hardy grasses, here recommended by Michelle D'Arcy, who operates Chicago-based Horticultural Associates, Inc. and specializes in landscape detail work.

Karl Foerster feather reed grass (*Calamagrostis arundinacea* 'Karl Foerster')
Stiff feather reed grass (*Calamagrostis acutiflora* 'Stricta')
Tufted hair grass (*Deschampsia caespitosa*)
Blue fescue (*Festuca glauca*)
Blue oat grass (*Helictotrichon sempervirens*)
Blue wild rye (*Leymus arenarius* 'Glaucus')
Silver variegated maiden grass (*Miscanthus sinensis* 'Morning Light')
Purple moor grass (*Molinia caerulea*)
Ribbon grass (*Phalaris arudinacea*)
Spodiopogon (*Spodiopogon sibiricus*)

"In Chicago, the windy city with little snow cover, winter lows to -20 degrees F, and wind chills down to -80 degrees F, many ornamental grasses previously thought to be hardy meet their premature demise during winter.

"We often find that in a grouping of the same species, some will make it through winter fine while beside them others from a different nursery will die. Having discussed this with growers, we've come to believe that some are grown from southern seed sources and are not as hardy as those propagated from northern strains. One secret to long-term success, then, is to find northern grown grasses."
Michelle D'Arcy, Horticultural Associates Inc.

NEIL DIBOLL'S SUGGESTED NATIVE PRAIRIE PLANTS

If mowing the lawn or maintaining an elaborate flower garden is taking too much of your time, perhaps you should consider replacing high-maintenance gardens with prairie plantings. Natural expanses of prairie grasses and wildflowers can create handsome displays with much less effort. Neil Diboll, consulting ecologist and CEO for Prairie Nursery, Inc., recommends the following for sandy (S), loam (L), or clay (C) soils in full sun.

FLOWERING PRAIRIE NATIVES

Butterfly weed (*Asclepias tuberosa*): S, L or var. Clay: L, C
Aster, smooth (*Aster laevis*): S, L
Indigo, white false (*Baptisia leucantha*): S, L, C
Indigo, cream false (*Baptisia leucophaea*): S, L
Shooting-star (*Dodecatheon meadia*): S, L (rich soil)
Coneflower, pale purple (*Echinacea pallida*): S, L, C
Coneflower, purple (*Echinacea purpurea*): S, L, C
Coneflower, yellow (*Echinacea pinnata*): S, L, C
Rattlesnake master (*Eryngium yuccifolium*): S, L, C
Queen-of-the-prairie (*Filipendula rubra*): S, L, C (rich soil)
Prairie smoke (*Geum triflorum*): S, L
Blazing-star, meadow (*Liatris ligulistylis*): L
Blazing-star, prairie (*Liatris pycnostachya*): S, L, C (rich soil)
Wild quinine (*Parthenium integrifolium*): S, L, C (rich soil)
Purple prairie clover (*Petalostemum purpureum*): S, L, C
Sweet black-eyed Susan (*Rudbeckia subtomentosa*): S, L, C (rich soil)
Compass plant (*Silphium laciniata*): S, L, C (rich soil)
Dock, prairie (*Silphium terebinthinaceum*): S, L, C (moist soil)
Goldenrod, Ohio (*Solidago ohioensis*): S, L, C (rich soil)
Goldenrod, stiff (*Solidago rigida*): S, L, C
Goldenrod, showy (*Solidago speciosa*): S, L
Culver's root (*Veronicastrum virginicum*): S, L, C (rich soil)
Golden alexanders, heartleaf (*Zizia aptera*): S, L, C (rich soil)

PRAIRIE GRASSES

Bluestem, little (*Schizachyrium scoparium*): S, L
Indian grass (*Sorghastrum nutans*): S, L, C
Prairie dropseed (*Sporobolus heterolepis*): S, L, C

"When we plant a prairie, we enter into a joint venture with nature. By creating a home for wild things, we incorporate the natural world into our world. This process creates a cooperative balance between people and nature in our own backyards. As an added bonus, a native prairie meadow requires far less maintenance than a typical lawn, so you save both time and money."
Neil Diboll, Prairie Nursery in Westfield, Wisconsin

"When it comes to hardiness, cities tend to be warmer than the countryside so gardeners living in Chicago can sometimes get by with plants that would usually grow farther south. But if a perennial fails, it may not be due entirely to a hardiness deficiency. There are many other important factors, like improper soil and site that also contribute. Our heavy clay soil can be particularly difficult."

Pam Wolfe, gardener in Downers Grove, Illinois, and author of Midwest Gardens, 200 Tips for Growing Vegetables in the Midwest *and* 200 Tips for Growing Flowers in the Midwest

Perennials through the Seasons

Take advantage of perennials two-faced nature—one smiling face in full flower for a portion of the growing season and one a resting face with foliage only—by planning a garden that will change with the seasons. You can develop entirely different color schemes as the seasons progress or maintain the same foundation colors with flowers that play up the appearance of your home indoors or out. The following list can help you plan ahead.

PERENNIALS THAT BLOOM SIX WEEKS OR LONGER

When starting a new perennial garden, use a professional landscaper's trick that will keep the garden interesting even as seasons change. Fill up to 50 percent of the garden with long-blooming perennials that flower six weeks to several months. While others come and go, the following perennials stay on the job (particularly if the old flowers are removed frequently).

Frikart's aster (*Aster Frikartii*)
Snowbank boltonia (*Boltonia asteroides* 'Snowbank')
Carpatican bellflower (*Campanula carpatica*)
Coreopsis (*Coreopsis* spp.)
Luxuriant bleeding heart (*Dicentra* × 'Luxuriant')
Purple coneflower (*Echinacea purpurea*)
Blanketflower (*Gaillardia* × *grandiflora*)
Lenten rose (*Helleborus orientalis*)
Reblooming daylilies (*Hemerocallis* 'Stella de Oro' and 'Happy Returns')
Perennial hibiscus (*Hibiscus Moscheutos*)
Bee balm (*Monarda didyma*)
Catmint (*Nepeta* spp.)
Orange coneflower (*Rudbeckia fulgida*)
Violet sage (*Salvia* × *superba* 'East Friesland' and 'May Night')
Scabiosa (*Scabiosa caucasica*)
Showy sedum (*Sedum spectabile*)
Stoke's aster (*Stokesia laevis*)
Rose verbena (*Verbena canadensis*)
Sunny Border Blue speedwell (*Veronica grandis* 'Sunny Border Blue')

A SAMPLER OF PERENNIAL BLOOM THROUGH THE SEASONS

Coordinating a sequence of bloom is one of the challenges and pleasures of perennial gardening. This sampler will help get you started. Expect some variation in bloom time depending on site, cultivar, and reblooming tendencies.

SPRING-BLOOMING PERENNIALS

Pasque flower (*Anemone Pulsatilla*)
Columbine (*Aquilegia* spp.)
Rock cress (*Arabis caucasica*)
False indigo (*Baptisia australis*)
Lily-of-the-valley (*Convallaria majalis*)
Pinks (*Dianthus* spp.)
Bleeding hearts (*Dicentra* spp.)
Crane's bill (*Geranium* spp.)
Christmas rose (*Helleborus niger*)
Lenten rose (*Helleborus orientalis*)
Candytuft (*Iberis sempervirens*)
Iris (*Iris* spp.)
Forget-me-not (*Myosotis sempervirens*)
Catmint (*Nepeta Faassenii*)
Peony (*Paeonia* hyb.)
Woodland phlox (*Phlox divaricata*)
Moss phlox (*Phlox subulata*)
Lungwort (*Pulmonaria saccharata*)
Meadow rue (*Thalictrum aquilegifolium*)
Foamflower (*Tiarella cordifolia*)
Sweet violet (*Viola odorata*)

Cardinal Flower

SUMMER-BLOOMING PERENNIALS

Yarrow (*Achillea* spp.)
Butterfly weed (*Asclepias tuberosa*)
Frikart's aster (*Aster* × *Frikartii*)
Astilbe (*Astilbe* spp.)
Plumbago (*Ceratostigma plumbaginoides*)
Coreopsis (*Coreopsis* spp.)
Purple coneflower (*Echinacea* spp.)
Blanket flower (*Gaillardia* × *grandiflora*)
Daylily (*Hemerocallis* spp)
Hostas (*Hosta* spp.)
Lavender (*Lavandula* spp.)
Shasta daisy (*Leucanthemum* × *superbum* syn. *Chrysanthemum superbum*)
Blazing star (*Liatris* spp.)
Ligularia (*Ligularia stenocephala* 'The Rocket')
Cardinal flower (*Lobelia cardinalis*)

Lupine (*Lupinus* × 'Russell Hybrids')
Husker Red penstemon (*Penstemon digitalis* 'Husker Red')
Russian sage (*Perovskia atriplicifolia*)
Early phlox (*Phlox maniculata*)
Garden phlox (*Phlox paniculata*)
Orange coneflower (*Rudbeckia* spp.)
Purple sage (*Salvia* × *superba*)

Japanese anemone (*Anemone* × *hybrida*)
Asters (*Aster* spp.)
Boltonia (*Boltonia* spp.)
Chrysanthemums (*Dendrathema* spp; syn. *Chrysanthemum* spp)
Sneezeweed (*Helenium autumnale*)
Maiden grass (*Miscanthus* spp.)
Showy sedum (*Sedum spectabile*)
Vera Jameson sedum (*Sedum* × 'Vera Jameson')
Toad lily (*Tricyrtis formosana*)

JOHN SCHULTZ'S CUT AND COME AGAIN PERENNIALS

Some perennials, if cut when first blooming, will turn around and flower again, qualities that John Schultz finds appealing. Schultz's family business, Garden Place, a mail-order perennial nursery in Mentor, Ohio, has acres of field-grown perennials and is a favorite summer stomping grounds of flower arrangers. Here are some of his recommendations.

Yarrows (*Achillea* spp.)
Bellflowers (*Campanula* spp.)
Cupid's dart (*Catananche caerulea*)
Border pinks (*Dianthus* spp.)
Coneflower, purple (*Echinacea purpurea*)
Globe thistle (*Echinops Ritro*)
Geraniums, hardy (*Geranium* spp.)
Perennial sunflower (*Helianthus* spp.)
Coralbells (*Heuchera* spp.)
Blazing star (*Liatris* spp.)
Russian sage (*Perovskia atriplicifolia*)
Coneflower, orange (*Rudbeckia* spp.)
Violet sage (*Salvia nemorosa*)
Sedum (*Sedum spectabile*)
Stoke's aster (*Stokesia laevis*)

LIBBY BRUCH'S FAVORITE AUTUMN PERENNIALS

Libby's wonderful nursery, Quailcrest Farm, in Wooster, Ohio, is a delightful place to roam in the fall when the gardens are full of lingering flowers, autumn foliage, and bright berries and pods. Here are some of the perennials that she shares with visitors and, now, with you.

Japanese anemone (*Anemone japonica*)	
Powis Castle artemisia (*Artemisia* × 'Powis Castle')	Silvery foliage
Italian arum (*Arum italicum*)	Red berries
Butterfly weed (*Asclepias tuberosa*)	Interesting pods
Asters (*Aster* spp.)	
Blackberry lily (*Belamcanda chinensis*)	Blackberry-like fruit
Snowbank boltonia (*Boltonia asteroides* 'Snowbank')	
Bluebeard (*Caryopteris* × *clandonensis* 'Dark Knight' and 'Longwood Blue')	
Turtlehead (*Chelone* spp.)	
Sweet autumn clematis (*Clematis paniculata*)	
Bright Star purple coneflower (*Echinacea purpurea* 'Bright Star')	
Joe-Pye weed (*Eupatorium purpureum*)	
Hardy ageratum (*Eupatorium coelestinum*)	
Spurge (*Euphorbia polychroma*)	
Gaura (*Gaura Lindheimeri*)	
Riverton Beauty sneezeweed (*Helenium autumnale* 'Riverton Beauty')	
Summer Sun heliopsis (*Heliopsis helianthoides* subsp. *scabra* 'Summer Sun')	
Peonies (*Paeonia* spp.)	Burgundy fall foliage
Russian sage (*Perovskia atriplicifolia*)	
Fairy rose (*Rosa* 'The Fairy')	
Autumn Joy sedum (*Sedum* × 'Autumn Joy')	

"Gone forever are the days when the beauty of May, June, and July gardens was followed by a period of garden boredom. No longer does autumn mean only mums and more mums. Certainly mums have their use for filling spots, but the number of lovely, colorful fall perennials available now makes autumn still another season of garden beauty and excitement.

"It would be remiss while talking about beauty in the fall not to mention some of the interesting and attractive shrubs and grasses such as red switch grass (*Panicum virgatum* 'Haense Hermes'), Virginia sweetspire (*Itea virginica*), winterberry (*Ilex verticillata*), and daphne (*Daphne* × *Burkwoodii* 'Carol Mackie')."
Libby Bruch, Quailcrest Farm, Wooster, Ohio

Perennials in the Landscape

In classic perennial borders, the shorter perennials lie in the front of the garden, the tallest at the back of the border, which builds in height like the silhouette of a far-off mountain. But the height progression of your perennials need not have the regimented regularity of a gymnasium bleacher; it can feature soft improvisations and natural irregularities.

Whether in a border or elsewhere in the landscape, perennials offer a blend of heights and forms, all of which can blend in pleasing diversity or fill a specific architectural function. The following lists are here to help you in this quest.

PERENNIALS WITH VERTICAL, SPIKED FLOWERS

Flowers borne on upright stems called spikes provide emphasis in a garden of mixed shapes. But too much of a good thing can make the garden look stiff and soldierly. Very tall and top-heavy spiked flowers may need staking.

Monkshood (*Aconitum* spp.)
Hollyhock (*Alcea rosea*)
Wild white indigo (*Baptisia alba*)
Wild blue indigo (*Baptisia australis*)
Black snakeroot (*Cimicifuga racemosa*)
Lucifer montebretia (*Crocosmia* × 'Lucifer')
Gas plant (*Dictamnus albus*)
Foxglove (*Digitalis* × *mertonensis*)
Dame's rocket (*Hesperis matronalis*)
Coralbells (*Heuchera sanguinea*)
Gayfeather (*Liatris* spp.)
Ligularia (*Ligularia stenocephala*)
Cardinal flower (*Lobelia cardinalis*)
Big blue lobelia (*Lobelia siphilitica*)
Lupine (*Lupinus* × Russell Hybrids)
Russian sage (*Perovskia* × *superba*)
False dragon-head (*Physostegia virginiana*)
Violet sage (*Salvia* × *superba*)
Mulleins (*Verbascum* spp.)
Veronicas (*Veronica* spp.)

Black Snakeroot

INVASIVE PLANTS

Where conditions are right, the following plants will spread, and spread, and spread—smothering out any lesser plants in their way. In a large informal garden or an isolated bed or planter, they can be enticing. Elsewhere they are aggravating to infuriating. Watch out for the following at plant exchanges, where their overburdened owners often try to pass them along to other, unsuspecting gardeners.

Goutweed (*Aegopodium Podagraria*)
White sage (*Artemisia ludoviciana*)
Chameleon plant (*Houttuynia cordata*)
Loosestrifes (*Lysimachia* spp.)
Purple loose strife (*Lythrum Salicaria*)
Plume poppy (*Macleaya cordata*)
Bee balm (*Monarda didyma*)
Obedient plant (*Physostegia virginiana*)
Canadian goldenrod (*Solidago canadensis*)
Periwinkle (*Vinca minor*)

PERENNIALS WITH VERTICAL FEATHERY FLOWERS

The following plants have softer looking, plumelike flowers.

Goat's beard (*Aruncus dioicus*)
Astilbe (*Astilbe × Arendsii*)
Queen-of-the-prairies (*Filipendula rubra*)
Meadow rue (*Thalictrum aquilegifolium*)

PERENNIALS WITH MOUNDED SHAPES

Perennials with rounded shapes make nice fillers in the garden and can mingle together into compatible sweeps and clusters that have more emphasis than a single plant.

Silver mound (*Artemisia Schmidtiana*)
Coreopsis (*Coreopsis* spp.)
Cottage pink (*Dianthus plumarius*)
Western bleeding heart (*Dicentra formosa* 'Luxuriant')
Blanketflower (*Gaillardia × grandiflora*)
Clark's geranium (*Geranium Clarkei*)
Johnson's Blue geranium (*Geranium ×* 'Johnson's Blue')
Sun rose (*Helianthemum nummularium*)
Coral bells (*Heuchera* spp.)
English lavender (*Lavandula angustifolia*)
Catmint (*Nepeta* spp.)
Peony (*Paeonia* spp.)
Autumn Joy sedum (*Sedum ×* 'Autumn Joy')
Vera Jameson sedum (*Sedum ×* 'Vera Jameson')

LOW PERENNIALS FOR GROUND COVER OR EDGING

Low perennials used in the foreground of the garden can be the most prominent elements, despite their small size.

For Sun
Bugleweed (*Ajuga* spp.)
Sea thrift (*Armeria maritima*)
Bergenia (*Bergenia* spp.)
Plumbago (*Ceratostigma plumbaginoides*)
Shepherd's Warning bloody cranesbill (*Geranium sanguineum*
    'Shepherd's Warning')
Dalmatian cranesbill (*Geranium dalmaticum*)
Candytuft (*Iberis sempervirens*)
Moss phlox (*Phlox subulata*)
Two-row sedum (*Sedum spurium*)

For Shade
European ginger (*Asarum europaeum*)

Bergenia (*Bergenia* spp.)
Golden star (*Chrysogonum virginianum*)
Epimedium (*Epimedium* spp.)
Sweet woodruff (*Galium odoratum*)
Bigroot geranium (*Geranium maculatum*)
Woodland phlox (*Phlox divaricata*)
Foamflowers (*Tiarella* spp.)
Violets (*Viola odorata*)

"Almost everything written about alpine hardiness is wrong. Most information has been taken from British or German books, which don't translate accurately to the Midwest. Many are quite winter hardy but struggle in summer heat. To find alpines well suited to your area, seek out a good grower and ask his advice. Some, such as gentians, that were almost impossible to grow in the past are now very growable if you just know how. Ask and you shall receive."
Bob Stewart, Arrowhead Alpines, Fowlerville, Michigan

MEGAN WOLFE'S MOST RELIABLE PERENNIALS

Megan Wolfe, landscape designer in Northwestern Indiana, likes high-performance perennials that can be counted on for a good flower display and long life.

Yarrows (*Achillea* spp.)
    Many sizes, shapes, and colors
Flowering onions (*Allium* spp.)
    They can punctuate the garden's flow
Silver Mound artemisia (*Artemisia Schmidtiana*)
    Less temperamental than lamb's ears
Moonbeam coreopsis (*Coreopsis verticillata* 'Moonbeam')
    Airy, substantial, and very classy
Purple coneflower (*Echinacea purpurea*)
    Good with other plants and in massed plantings
Daylilies (*Hemerocallis* spp.)
    Especially the long bloomers
Coralbells (*Heuchera micrantha*)
    Bronze foliage for contrast
Siberian irises (*Iris sibirica*)
    Can take a little shade
Johnson's Blue hardy geranium (*Geranium* × 'Johnson's Blue')
    It's small, blue, and everything the others aren't
Coneflowers (*Rudbeckia* spp.)
    Tough customers and cheerful

ROY KLEHM'S FAVORITE PEONIES, MIDWESTERN CLASSICS

Roy Klehm, a third-generation peony breeder from the greater Chicago area, specializes in peonies, peonies, and more peonies. He has been concentrating on developing peonies with new and richer flower colors. Among the most exciting are unique coral-flowered peonies, first developed by a chemist who cracked the color barrier by analyzing petal colors and hybridizing parent plants with the most coral pigment saturation. For rich pink and coral peonies, look for the following.

> 'Angel Cheeks'
> 'Chiffon Clouds'
> 'Moonstone'
> 'Pillowtalk'
> 'Pink Lemonade'
> 'Pink Coral'
> 'Coral Charm'
> 'Coral Sunset'
> 'Coral Supreme'
> 'Pink Hawaiian Coral'

"Peonies are a perennial that's particularly well suited to the Midwest and won't grow well in the hot South. Once established in rich, well-drained soil, peonies can live for decades. At my former 1950s home outside Cleveland, an old hedge of softly fragrant white peonies thrived in the front yard. When we had to excavate nearby for septic repairs, the roots reached over ten feet deep through dense clay, a particularly remarkable accomplishment."
Susan McClure

"Peony roots go way down, especially when planted in rich, heavy soil. They're there to stay, and that's why peonies live so long. They are very permanent plants that can establish their territories and defend themselves."
Roy Klehm, Klehm Nursery

PERENNIALS FOR CRACKS AND CREVICES

When planted between a rock and a hard place, some perennials thrive. They billow out, cascade over stone retaining walls and creep along the openings between stones or bricks in a walk. In such a setting, silhouetted against a blank canvas of stone, brick, or cement, they are particularly appealing and add a soft grace to the garden. Some plants suitable for cracks and crevices include the following.

> Woolly yarrow (*Achillea tomentosa*)
> Bugleweed (*Ajuga* spp.)
> Rock cress (*Arabis caucasica*)

Sea pink (*Armeria maritima*)
Aubrieta (*Aubrieta deltoidea*)
Serbian bellflower (*Campanula Poscharskyana*)
Snow-in-summer (*Cerastium tomentosum*)
Pinks (*Dianthus* spp.)
Poor Robin's plantain (*Erigeron pulchellus*)
Candytuft (*Iberis sempervirens*)
Creeping sedums (*Sedum* spp.)
Hen-and-chicks (*Sempervivum tectorum*)
Sweet violet (*Viola odorata*)

PERENNIALS THAT ATTRACT HUMMINGBIRDS

That quiet drone you may sometimes hear within my garden is not someone's cellular phone acting up but the rapidly beating wings of a hummingbird as it hovers to capture nectar. Although hummingbirds are not particularly common, if you plant one of the following favorites, your chances of seeing one are very good.

Wild columbine (*Aquilegia canadensis*)
Butterfly weed (*Asclepias tuberosa*)
Coralbells (*Heuchera sanguinea*)
Cardinal flower (*Lobelia cardinalis*)
Bee balm (*Monarda didyma*)

PERENNIALS THAT ATTRACT BUTTERFLIES

While enjoying the beauty of a perennial garden, why not feed butterflies too? They sip nectar from certain flowers, fluttering like living blossoms from bloom to bloom. If butterfly gardening is your game, avoid using pesticides that will do them harm.

Butterfly weed (*Asclepias tuberosa*)
Asters (*Aster* spp.)
Wild indigo (*Baptisia australis*)
Red valerian (*Centranthus ruber*)
Pinks (*Dianthus* spp.)
Purple coneflower (*Echinacea purpurea*)
Joe-Pye weed (*Eupatorium purpurea*)
Sneezeweed (*Helenium* spp.)
Perennial sunflower (*Helianthus multiflorus*)
Coral bell (*Heuchera* spp.)
Gayfeather (*Liatris* spp.)
Bee balm (*Monarda didyma*)
Phlox (*Phlox* spp.)
Roses (*Rosa* spp.)
Orange coneflower (*Rudbeckia fulgida*)
Violet sage (*Salvia* × *superba*)
Stonecrop (*Sedum* spp.)
Goldenrod (*Solidago* spp.)
Speedwell (*Veronica* spp.)

PERENNIALS FOR CUTTING

Enjoying perennial flowers outdoors in the garden is all well and good, but bringing some into the house to keep in a vase on the kitchen counter is even better. You can see them up close and personal and allow those with fragrance (marked with an asterisk) to perfume the house. In the case of lilies and peonies, some cultivars are more aromatic than others.

LONG-STEM CUTTING PERENNIALS
For tall vases and big bouquets

Yarrow (*Achillea* spp.)
Alkanet (*Anchusa azurea*)
Butterfly weed (*Asclepias tuberosa*)
Asters (*Aster* spp.)
Astilbe (*Astilbe* spp.)
Wild indigo (*Baptisia australis*)
Peach leaf bellflower (*Campanula persicifolia*)
Perennial cornflower (*Centaurea montana*)
*Red valerian (*Centranthus ruber*)
Lance leaf coreopsis (*Coreopsis lanceolata*)
Purple coneflowers (*Echinacea* spp.)
Globe thistle (*Echinops Ritro*)
Sea holly (*Eryngium amethystinum*)
Perennial sunflower (*Helianthus multiflorus*)
*Fragrant hostas (*Hosta* hyb. 'Royal Standard', 'Honeybells',
    'Fragrant Bouquet', and 'So Sweet')
Iris (*Iris* spp.)
*Lilies (*Lilium* spp.)
Lupines (*Lupinus* hyb.)
Shasta daisies (*Leucanthemum* × *superbum*; syn. *Chrysanthemum* × *superbum*)
Gayfeather (*Liatris* spp.)
*Bee balm (*Monarda* spp.)
Russian sage (*Perovskia atriplicifolia*)
*Peony (*Paeonia* hyb.)
Phlox (*Phlox* spp.)
*Rose (*Rosa* hyb.)
Coneflowers (*Rudbeckia* spp.)
Violet sage (*Salvia* × *superba*)

SHORT-STEM CUTTING PERENNIALS
For bud vases, corsages, and tussie mussies

Columbine (*Aquilegia* spp.)
Sea thrift (*Armeria* spp.)
Carpatican bellflower (*Campanula carpatica*)
Chrysanthemums (*Chrysanthemum* spp.)
*Pinks (*Dianthus* spp.)
Blanket flower (*Gaillardia* spp.)

Coralbells (*Heuchera* spp.)
*Catmint (*Nepeta* spp.)
Pincushion flower (*Scabiosa caucasica*)
*Sweet violet (*Viola odorata*)

PERENNIALS WITH SEEDS THAT BIRDS LOVE

To most wild birds, flowers are inconsequential—their real interest begins when perennials set seeds. This is when colorful goldfinches and tuxedoed chickadees begin darting around the garden, plucking at mature seed heads. To enjoy this scene, let seed heads ripen and be patient if plants are not as perfectly groomed as they otherwise would be.

Asters (*Aster* spp.)
Boltonia (*Boltonia asteroides*)
Coreopsis (*Coreopsis* spp.)
Purple coneflower (*Echinacea purpurea*)
Globe thistle (*Echinops Ritro*)
Shasta daisy (*Leucanthemum* × *superbum*; syn. *Chrysanthemum* × *superbum*)
Orange coneflower (*Rudbeckia* spp.)
Goldenrod (*Solidago* spp.)
Iron weed (*Vernonia noveboracensis*)

ALPINE PLANTS TO TRY

Growing alpines, little gems that naturally grow on mountainsides, is a delightful occupation for many a Midwestern rock gardener. Bob Stewart, owner of Arrowhead Alpines in Fowlerville, Michigan, has grown hundreds of species ranging from simple to difficult. Here is a list of his favorites, all extremely desirable plants that should be more widely grown. Few alpine plants have common names, so this list includes only botanical names.

Androsace Vandellii	*Nomocharis Ferrari*
Briggsia muscicola	*Origanum amanum*
Campanula Zoysii	*Primula sonchifolia*
Dicentra peregrina	*Raoulia australis*
Edrianthus pumilio	*Saxifraga diapensioides*
Fuchsia magellanica	*Telesonix Jamesii*
Gentiana Ferrari	*Umbilicus rupestris*
Haberlea rhodopensis	*Viola coronifera* (rosulate)
Iris Nicholi	*Waldheimia tomentosa*
Jankaea Heldreichii	*Xeronema Callistemon*
Kelseya uniflora	*Zauschneria Garrettii*
Lewisia Tweedyi	
Mutisia spinosa	

FERNS

In shady, older neighborhoods or around houses built into the woods, ferns can reign supreme. Most thrive where sun is scarce, produce handsome greenery in bold upright or soft sprawling shapes, and make interesting companions for more ordinary shade dwellers like hostas and impatiens. Although a primitive form of plant that produces spores instead of seeds, some ferns are exceptionally hardy. Lady ferns (*Athyrium Filix-femina*) and wood ferns (*Dryopteris dilatatum*), for instance, can grow as far north as Alaska, making surviving Midwestern winters a breeze.

People who have dabbled with ferns know that each species has its own personality and appearance, although sometimes the differences may be so subtle that only a dedicated fern-follower can easily make the distinction. Lady ferns and wood ferns both have lacy, highly divided fronds that are almost identical. The difference lies in the overall frond shape. Wood fern fronds are triangular with long barren stem bases, while lady fern fronds have a diamond silhouette.

Other ferns are very distinctive. The Japanese painted fern (*Athyrium nipponicum* 'Pictum'), with silver highlighted fronds, is a bright ornamental with plenty of pizzazz. Although ferns don't flower—they produce spores on frond undersides or on separate stalks—some outstanding species send up reproductive stalks that resemble emphatic, bronze flower spikes.

American native ferns, by far, monopolize the Midwestern garden market, but a few introductions from Europe, the Orient, and elsewhere, or cultivars developed for leaf color or interesting frond configurations can be found. New ferns, although much less common than new perennials, are the province of specialty growers such as the Lundberg Nursery.

Lady Fern

Right Plant, Right Place

If you've ever seen the soft, spongy soil of a forest floor (the most spectacular in my memory being in the climax beech-maple forest at Hueston Woods in Oxford, Ohio), you've got a good idea of the kind of soil ferns prefer. Where deciduous leaves fall and decay, the soil tends to be rich, moist, and often on the acidic side. Perfect for ferns. Where soils are hard, dry, and devoid of organic material, buy bulk loads of compost and add plenty before planting. With a good start in good soil, some ferns can be transplanted out of their woodland environment and into the garden. Here are some examples.

FERNS TOLERANT OF SUN

Whenever an author attempts to categorize a group of plants as shade-loving, some adventuresome species inevitably comes out of the woodwork and grow in the sun. Such is the case with ferns. You might see the following ferns peeking out of the woods or thriving in a morning of sun on the east side of the house.

Lady fern (*Athyrium Filix-femina*)
Japanese painted fern (*Athyrium nipponicum* 'Pictum')
Hay-scented fern (*Dennstaedtia punctilobula*)
Male fern (*Dryopteris Filix-mas*)
Cinnamon fern (*Osmunda cinnamomea*)
Interrupted fern (*Osmunda Claytoniana*)
Royal fern (*Osmunda regalis*)

Cinnamon
Fern

FERNS FOR DROUGHT TOLERANCE

Young and newly planted ferns, like most plants, will need watering when dry weather strikes, but some mature ferns can withstand moderately dry weather without additional irrigation. If you have a precarious well or live in an area with summer watering bans, consider planting one of the following. (Cautionary note: Bracken fern is an aggressive spreader.)

Male fern (*Dryopteris Filix-mas*)
Fancy fern (*Dryopteris intermedia*)
Marginal wood fern (*Dryopteris marginalis*)
Interrupted fern (*Osmunda Claytoniana*)
Christmas fern and kin (*Polystichum* spp.)
Bracken fern (*Pteridium aquilinum*)
Cliff fern (*Woodsia obtusa*)

FERNS FOR WET LOCATIONS

Few plants, with the notable exception of the following ferns, grow well in a boggy location. Where you have wet shade throughout the growing season, these ferns are a natural. But don't let the area dry out in summer or the ferns may fade into premature dormancy.

Lady fern (*Athyrium Filix-femina*)
Ostrich fern (*Matteuccia Struthiopteris*)

Sensitive fern (*Onoclea sensibilis*)
Cinnamon fern (*Osmunda cinnamomea*)
Royal fern (*Osmunda regalis*)

FERNS FOR SLIGHTLY ALKALINE LOCATIONS

Most ferns do best in slightly acidic soil, but much of the Midwest is alkaline. Rather than continually adjusting the soil pH with sulfur, accept the inevitable and plant ferns that will accept a sweet, native soil.

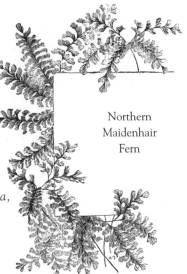

Northern
Maidenhair
Fern

Northern maidenhair fern (*Adiantum pedatum*)
Maidenhair spleenwort (*Asplenium trichomanes*)
Ebony spleenwort (*Asplenium platyneuron*)
Wood ferns (*Dryopteris carthusiana, D. dilatata, D. expansa*)
Ostrich fern (*Matteuccia Struthiopteris*)
Interrupted fern (*Osmunda Claytoniana*)
Marsh fern (*Thelypteris palustris*)

NEW AND BETTER HARDY FERNS FROM JEAN AND SCOTT LUNDBERG

Always scanning the horizon for exciting new ferns, Scott and Jean Lundberg, from Lundberg Nursery, a wholesale fern specialist in Niles, Michigan, shared their list of favorite hardy ferns from around the world. If you're looking for trend-setting fern gardens, consider growing one of the following.

English painted or eared lady fern (*Athyrium otophorum*)
Spinulose lady (*Athyrium spinulosum*)
Maidenhair spleenwort (*Asplenium trichomanes*)
Western maidenhair (*Adiantum aleuticum*)
Himalayan or evergreen maidenhair (*Adiantum venustum*)
Golden scaled male (*Dryopteris affinis*)
Amur wood fern (*Dryopteris amurensis*)
Spinulose wood fern (*Dryopteris austriaca*)
Log fern (*Dryopteris celsa*)
Champion's wood fern (*Dryopteris Championii*)
Broad buckler fern (*Dryopteris dilatata*)
Autumn fern (*Dryopteris erythrosora*)
Male fern (*Dryopteris Filix-mas*)
Goldie's fern (*Dryopteris Goldiana*)
Hart's tongue fern (*Phyllitis Scolopendrium*)
Alaska fern (*Polystichum setiferum divisilobum*)
Korean rock fern (*Polystichum tsus-simense*)
Braun's holly fern (*Polystichum Braunii*)
Makino's fern (*Polystichum makinoi*)

"We got started in the fern business as enthusiastic amateur collectors and still enjoy finding new ferns. Of the hundreds of temperate zone ferns, only a dozen or so are commonly used. Our personal favorites include Himalayan maidenhair (*Adiantum venustum*), which forms mounds of delicately cut fronds; spinulose lady fern (*Athyrium spinulosum*) from the Orient with its elegant shape; hart's tongue (*Phyllitis Scolopendrium*), with its many cultivars and strap shaped fronds; and English painted fern (*Athyrium otophorum*), which has lime green new foliage and striking maroon stems."

Scott and Jean Lundberg, Lundberg Nursery, Niles, Michigan

Ferns through the Seasons

Although ferns do not put on the lavish seasonal displays of daylilies, viburnums, or crabapples, they do offer some variety though the seasons and particularly in winter.

EVERGREEN FERNS

These are nature's gift to the winter garden. Billowing forest green on a snowy bank when everything else is gray and brown, they provide a reminder that spring will again return. Groom evergreen ferns in early spring, removing tattered leaves so a fresh new fan can appear.

Maidenhair spleenwort (*Asplenium trichomanes*)
Shield fern (*Dryopteris austriaca*)
Fancy fern (*Dryopteris intermedia*)
Male fern (*Dryopteris Filix-mas*)
Rock fern (*Polypodium virginianum*)
Christmas fern (*Polystichum acrostichoides*)

Male Fern

Ferns do not flower like roses and lilies. Instead, they produce spores, a complicated and primitive system for reproduction. Ripe spores, produced beneath fronds or on their own fertile stems, fall to the damp ground and develop into tiny green patches called *gametophytes*. Gametophytes produce either male or female reproductive elements. When the weather is wet and the gametophytes are primed, the male elements swim to the female and fertilization takes place. A new fern arises directly out of the female gametophyte.

PERSISTENT FERTILE FRONDS FOR WINTER INTEREST

Some ferns separate their fertile stems from their leaves, allowing the tightly sculpted spore-generating structures to stand out amid the softer fronds. Some remain at attention, even in winter, adding interest to the winter garden and catching the snow in picturesque ways.

Ostrich fern (*Matteuccia Struthiopteris*)
Sensitive fern (*Onoclea sensibilis*)
Cinnamon fern (*Osmunda cinnamomea*)

Ferns in the Landscape

Ferns are a natural companion for a woodland garden of wildflowers or a shade garden of ivy and daffodils. Their fronds provide interest even when the trilliums and anemones are long gone. But ferns need not be stereotyped into woodland settings. With a little imagination, you can find other settings where they will delight, as in a foundation planting or a rock garden. Consider species appearance and growth habits to get a full understanding of what a particular plant may be able to do.

FERNS FOR GROUND COVER

These ferns creep on spreading rhizomes and can cover ground in large, lush colonies. Except unstoppable bracken fern, other creeping ferns may not be aggressive enough to crowd out weeds. Expect to help them with a hoe from time to time.

Lady fern (*Athyrium Filix-femina*)
Hay-scented fern (*Dennstaedtia punctilobula*)
Glade fern (*Diplazium pycnocarpon*)
Sensitive fern (*Onoclea sensibilis*)
Bracken fern (*Pteridium aquilinum*)
Virginia chain fern (*Woodwardia virginica*)

Sensitive Fern

LACY FRONDED FERNS

These are the classic ferns, so highly divided that they appear cut from green lace; beautiful from afar and even more outstanding up close.

Lady fern (*Athyrium Filix-femina*)
Fragile fern (*Cystopteris fragilis*)
Hay-scented fern (*Dennstaedtia punctilobula*)
Shield fern (*Dryopteris austriaca*)
Wood fern (*Dryopteris dilatatum*)
Male fern (*Dryopteris Filix-mas*)
Oak fern (*Gymnocarpium Dryopteris*)
Northern beech fern (*Thelypteris connectilis*)
Soft shield fern (*Polystichum setiferum*)

RUSSELL STAFFORD ON FERNS

Russell Stafford, head of horticulture at Fernwood Botanic Garden in Niles, Michigan, and former horticultural program coordinator and editor for the Center for Plant Conservation at the Arnold Arboretum, is an avid fernophile who is apt to spread his love of the plants to you.

"Ferns are often typecast as shade garden bit players, valuable only as a foil to flowering woodland plants. Yet they can play starring as well as supporting roles in both shade and sun. For example, the bold foliage, running rootstock, and sun tolerance of sensitive fern (*Onoclea sensibilis*) make it an ideal large-scale ground cover. Adaptable to boggy condition as in Zone 3 temperatures, it rapidly spreads to form lush, knee-high colonies in all but the most difficult sites and blends beautifully with other US native and naturalized wetlands plants such as yellow flag (*Iris Pseudacorus*) and western bog arum (*Lysichiton americanum*). Similarly, hay-scented fern (*Dennstaedtia punctilobula*), although too vigorous for the small garden, is unexcelled for covering ground in woodland openings and edges. An astonishingly adaptable native, it thrives in most soils in sun or shade, weathers Zone 3 winters, and is unpalatable to deer. I also love the wistful, earthy scent of its withering fronds—the smell of the eastern woods in fall.

"Beauty and adaptability also characterize the ferns of the genus *Osmunda*. The fuzzy fiddleheads and whirled, arching sterile fronds of cinnamon fern (*O. cinnamomea*) are—to my mind—the quintessence of fernness. (The fertile fronds, however, are anything but fernlike, their cinnamon stick stipes terminating in plumes of clustered spores.) Native to North American swamps, it does well in damp soils in shade or sun, where it attains heights of thirty inches or more and complements the bold leaves of false hellebore (*Veratrum viride*) and umbrella leaf (*Darmera peltata*). Similar in culture, effect, and hardiness (Zone 3) to cinnamon fern but unaccountably spurned by gardeners, interrupted fern (*O. Claytoniana*) earns its common name by bearing its spore clusters midway on an otherwise ferny frond. It deserves wider use.

"In contrast, few ferns are as unfernlike as royal fern (*O. regalis*). In damp soils, the majestic fronds—which resemble locust leaves—can reach upwards of four feet, dominating the wetland perennial garden (and warranting combination with other lordly moisture lovers such as *Rodgersia* and *Ligularia*). Equally laudable are its bronzy spring and fall foliage, sun tolerance, and extreme hardiness (to Zone 2).

"The deservedly popular Christmas fern (*Polystichum acrostichoides*) does just about everything but tolerate sun. A long-lived evergreen (and hardy to Zone 4), it is sturdy enough to cover a bank and elegant enough to serve as a specimen, its dark, leathery, two-foot fronds standing in splendid contrast to the delicate foliage and flowers of fernleaf bleeding heart (*Dicentra eximia*) and yellow fumitory (*Corydalis lutea*).

"Speaking of *Polystichum*, the frills and ruffles of soft shield fern (*Polystichum setiferum*) are among the marvels of the shade garden. In some forms, such as 'Divisilobum', the dusky green fronds are so finely feathered that I can never resist touching them. These evergreens deserve a starring role in the garden, set off perhaps by coarse leaved companions such as lungworts (*Pulmonaria*) and navelwort (*Omphalodes cappadocica*). Belying their delicate appearance, they will tolerate dryish soils and Zone 5 conditions.

"Also improbably tough, the Himalayan maidenhair (*Adiantum venustum*) succeeds into Zone 5, spreading in shady, sheltered sites to form low, lacy carpets. It works well in large rock gardens or in ground cover tapestries, interwoven with the likes of crested iris (*Iris cristata*) and Allegheny spurge (*Pachysandra procumbens*).

"Some ferns are simply too colorful to relegate to supporting roles. The emerging spring foliage of ghost fern (*Athyrium otophorum*) is like a shaft of sunlight in the shade garden, its frosted lime tones contrasting beautifully with the burgundies, silvers, and bronzes of Japanese painted fern (*Athyrium nipponicum* 'Pictum'). The purple-striped, two-foot fronds mature to light green. A relative newcomer to Midwest gardens, ghost fern is proving hardy into Zone 5. Equally colorful are the coppery young fronds of autumn fern (*Dryopteris erythrosora*), which later darken to a glossy leathery green. Well suited as a specimen plant for moist, semishaded sites into Zone 5 (or in a cool greenhouse), the clump-forming two-footer combines effectively with woodland carpeters such as Canadian ginger (*Asarum canadense*) and foamflower (*Tiarella* spp.).

"Rather than frail shade garden fillers, these and many other ferns are sturdy, versatile ornamentals that offer limitless but often unexploited possibilities. En mass or as specimens, ferns are unexcelled for adding character and tone to shady—and sunny—gardens."

TALL FERNS

Taller ferns erupting from low-growing ground covers look like sparkling fountains of greenery. Big and bold, they make powerful statements in the landscape.

> Giant wood fern (*Dryopteris Goldiana*)
> Ostrich fern (*Matteuccia Struthiopteris*)
> Interrupted fern (*Osmunda Claytoniana*)
> Royal fern (*Osmunda regalis*)

FERNS WITH COLORFUL OR CRESTED FOLIAGE

Plant breeders continue to push species to their limits of genetic flexibility, turning ferns into curling, crested, or silver-touched garden pleasers. These fancy fronded cultivars can be a special feature in a perennial garden but may not be in keeping in a conservative native plant collection.

> Japanese painted fern (*Athyrium nipponicum* 'Pictum')
> Fancy Fronds lady fern (*Athyrium Filix-femina* 'Fancy Fronds')
> Barnesii male fern (*Dryopteris Filix-mas* 'Barnesii')
> Cristata Martindale male fern (*Dryopteris Filix-mas* 'Cristata Martindale')
> Purpurescens royal fern (*Osmunda regalis* var. *regalis* 'Purpurescens')

ANNUALS

Annual flowers are the superheros of the Midwestern landscape. Cold-hardy pansies, with suits of vivid blue emblazoned with gold and capes of scarlet, fight a never-ending battle for spring color. Heat-loving annuals, like petunias with their languid clumps of floppy brimmed flowers, can bloom nonstop from summer to frost, surpassing even the longest blooming shrub or tree.

Annuals can go where few other flowers dare to tread. Graceful taller annuals like cleome and cosmos fill the void around threadbare shrubs or the awkward spots between newly planted perennials. Lower growing annuals like sweet alyssum and pansies cover sorrowful spaces left as spring bulbs fade. Everywhere there is an opening in the garden, there is an annual well suited to filling it.

Describing annuals as everbloomers with all virtue and no vice is a bit misleading, however. When hard hit by Midwestern summer heat, cool-season annuals like pansies, sweet alyssum, lobelia, and calendula may stop blooming or worse. The frothy, billowing displays of warm-season annuals—grandiflora petunias, nasturtiums, and salvias that drew so many wonderful comments in June—may fade in summer to become more of a distraction than an attraction. Cutting back scraggly stems by one-third and providing extra water and fertilizer can restore good health and vigorous new bloom for many annuals.

For a small number of annuals, however, efforts at restoration are in vain. Sunflowers, China asters, and baby's breath provide only one glorious bout of bloom and then are through. For extended bloom, plant new seeds or seedlings every couple weeks through early summer.

Right Plant, Right Place

Annuals only live up to their merits if provided with good growing conditions. Shoving even the most vigorous begonia into rock-hard ground amid overgrown yews is unlikely to prove satisfying. But give most annuals sufficient light and fertile well-drained soil, and they will flourish. Not every garden site will be perfect. Use careful species selection to make up for exposure inadequacies.

ANNUALS FOR SHADE

A large number of annuals will grow in either sun or partial sun, a versatility garnered in breeder's laboratories and much welcomed in the mature yard. Where shade is more intense, however, the selection wanes. Although some annuals may survive, they often lunge for the sun, creating odd and uninspiring silhouettes. Should this be the case in your yard, consider whether an ivy or periwinkle ground cover would be a better alternative to annuals.

ANNUALS FOR SUN OR LIGHT SHADE

Ageratum (*Ageratum Houstonianum*)
Summer forget-me-not (*Anchusa capensis*)
Begonias, wax leaf (*Begonia semperflorens-cultorum*)
Browallia (*Browallia speciosa*)
Vinca (*Catharanthus roseus*)
Coleus (*Coleus* × *hybridus*)
Foxy foxglove (*Digitalis purpurea* `Foxy')
New Guinea impatiens (*Impatiens* hyb.)
Balsam (*Impatiens Balsamina*)
Edging lobelia (*Lobelia Erinus*)
Sweet alyssum (*Lobularia maritima*)
Baby blue-eyes (*Nemophila Menziesii*)
Nierembergia (*Nierembergia hippomanica*)
Annual phlox (*Phlox Drummondii*)
Mealy cup salvia (*Salvia farinacea*)
Butterfly flower (*Schizanthus* × *wisetonensis*)
Wishbone flower (*Torenia Fournieri*)
Vinca vine (*Vinca major* 'Variegata')
Johnny jump-up (*Viola tricolor*)
Pansy (*Viola* × *Wittrockiana*)

Begonia

ANNUALS FOR MEDIUM SHADE

Begonia (*Begonia semperflorens-cultorum*)
Browallia (*Browallia speciosa*)
Coleus (*Coleus* × *hybridus*)
Monkey flower (*Mimulus* × *hybridus*)
Forget-me-nots (*Myosotis sylvatica*)
Impatiens (*Impatiens Wallerana*)
Wishbone flower (*Torenia Fournieri*)

ANNUALS FOR DRY CONDITIONS

A summer drought is the norm in most parts of the Midwest. But where the soil is well drained, sandy, or sloped, the garden may be dry most of the year. This is the ideal place for drought tolerant annuals or species that detest wet feet and grow soft, sloppy, and overfed in moist, rich soils.

Vinca (*Catharanthus rosea*)
Cockscomb (*Celosia cristata*)
Spider flower (*Cleome Hasslerana*)
Calliopsis (*Coreopsis tinctoria*)

Cosmos (*Cosmos sulphureus* and *bipinnatus*)
Snow-on-the-mountain (*Euphorbia marginata*)
Blanket flower (*Gaillardia pulchella*)
Gazania (*Gazania rigens*)
Globe amaranth (*Gomphrena* spp.)
Medallion melampodium (*Melampodium paludosum*
 'Medallion')
Nierembergia (*Nierembergia hippomanica*)
Moss rose (*Portulaca grandiflora*)
Gloriosa daisy (*Rudbeckia hirta*)
Red sage (*Salvia coccinea*)
Creeping zinnia (*Sanvitalia procumbens*)
Mexican sunflower (*Tithonia rotundifolia*)
Garden verbena (*Verbena* × *hybrida*)

Vinca

ANNUALS FOR MOIST SOIL

Where soils are generously moist throughout the growing season look for annuals that like lush conditions. When moist soils are accompanied by poor drainage, however, annuals are likely to suffer from rots.

Abelmoschus (*Abelmoschus moschatus*)
Love-lies-bleeding (*Amaranthus caudatus*)
Browallia (*Browallia speciosa*)
Globe amaranth (*Gomphrena globosa*)
Impatiens (*Impatiens Wallerana*)
Moonflower (*Ipomoea alba*)
Morning glory (*Ipomoea purpurea*)
Garden forget-me-not (*Myosotis sylvatica*)

ANNUALS FOR ALKALINE SOIL

Where the soil pH creeps up a little high, like the blood pressure of an anxious executive, the solution is easy. Grow annuals that don't mind moderately sweet soils.

Bachelor's button (*Centaurea Cyanus*)
Spider flower (*Cleome Hasslerana*)
Larkspur (*Consolida* spp.)
Dahlberg daisy (*Dyssodia tenuiloba*)
California poppy (*Escholzia californica*)
Lisianthus (*Eustoma grandiflorum*)
Blanket flower (*Gaillardia pulchella*)
Globe amaranth (*Gomphrena globosa*)
Sweet alyssum (*Lobularia maritima*)
Stock (*Matthiola incana*)
Love-in-a-mist (*Nigella damascena*)
Annual phlox (*Phlox Drummondii*)
Gloriosa daisy (*Rudbeckia hirta*)
Mexican sunflower (*Tithonia rountidifolia*)
Zinnia (*Zinnia* spp.)

Annuals through the Seasons

Despite their propensity for long bloom, annuals are still plants and not machines. Some do better in the cool, mild stretches of spring and fall. Others thrive in the summer sun. Knowing what to expect from any given annual is the start to coaxing it to burst into bloom and stay in bloom when you need it most.

TENDER SUMMER ANNUALS

While the previous annuals brave temperatures dipping briefly below freezing, these tender annuals turn into limp piles of greenery in the cold. Truly tropical, they shouldn't go outside until all danger of frost is past.

Ageratum (*Ageratum Houstonianum*)
Fibrous rooted begonia (*Begonia sempervirens*)
Browallia (*Browallia speciosa*)
Canna (*Canna* × *generalis*)
Cockscomb (*Celosia cristata*)
Cosmos (*Cosmos* spp.)
Coleus (*Coleus* × *hybridus*)
Flowering tobacco (*Nicotiana alata*)
Fuschia (*Fuschia* × *hybrida*)
Gazania (*Gazania linearis*)
Globe amaranth (*Gomphrena globosa*)
Sunflower (*Helianthus annuus*)
Impatiens (*Impatiens* spp.)
Lantana (*Lantana Camara*)
Marigold (*Tagetes* spp.)
Geraniums (*Pelargonium* × *hortorum* and *G. peltatum*)
Petunia (*Petunia* × *hybrida*)
Salvia (*Salvia splendens*)
Creeping zinnia (*Sanvitalia procumbens*)
Zinnia (*Zinnia* spp.)

FROST-HARDY SPRING AND FALL ANNUALS

Early- and late-season bloomers may be the dearest to the Midwesterner's heart, particularly when the revels of summer retreat and these plants remain stalwartly flowering. In the lower Midwest, hardy annuals such as pansies can be planted in early fall for flowers the moment spring dawns.

Bachelor's Button

Snapdragons (*Antirrhinum majus*)
Pot marigold (*Calendula officinalis*)
Bachelor's button (*Centaurea Cyanus*)
Dusty miller (*Cineraria* spp.)
Pinks (*Dianthus chinensis*)
Lobelia (*Lobelia Erinus*)

Sweet alyssum (*Lobularia maritima*)
Sweet peas (*Lathyrus odoratus*)
Johnny jump-up (*Viola tricolor*)
Pansies (*Viola* × *Wittrockiana*)

CHICAGO BOTANIC GARDEN SUMMER FLOWERING ANNUALS TRIALS

In 1994, the Chicago Botanic Garden evaluated fifty-five summer flowering annuals for flower size and color, plant size, peak bloom, and pest and disease problems. The following rated excellent and were highly recommended.

Black-eyed
Susan

Anise hyssop (*Agastache anisata*)
Parasol vinca (*Catharanthus roseus* 'Parasol')
Pretty in Rose vinca (*Catharanthus roseus* 'Pretty in Rose')
Elfin herb (*Cuphea hyssopifolia* 'Desert Snow')
Floral Lace Purple China pink (*Dianthus* 'Floral Lace Purple')
Ideal Violet China pink (*Dianthus chinensis* 'Ideal Violet')
Telstar Pink China pink (*Dianthus chinensis* 'Telstar Pink')
Hare's tail grass (*Lagurus ovatus*)
Lady lavender (*Lavandula angustifolia* 'Lady')
Flowering tobacco (*Nicotiana sylvestris*)
Celebrity Chiffon Morn petunia (*Petunia* 'Celebrity Chiffon Morn')
Purple Wave petunia (*Petunia* 'Purple Wave')
Indian Summer coneflower (*Rudbeckia hirta* 'Indian Summer')
Valentine Light Blue verbena (*Verbena* × *hybrida* 'Valentine Light Blue')

FLOWERS TO DIRECT SOW

There are more ways to grow flowers than simply buying flats in a greenhouse on Memorial Day. One inexpensive alternative to ten-dollar flats are seed packets. When sown directly in the garden, quick-growing and early-flowering annuals can give elegant results.

FOR MIDSPRING PLANTING
Bachelor's button (*Centaurea Cyanus*)
Sweet pea (*Lathyrus odoratus*)
Love-in-a-mist (*Nigella damascena*)
Annual poppies (*Papaver* spp.)

FOR LATE-SPRING OR EARLY-SUMMER PLANTING
Cosmos (*Cosmos* spp.)
Globe amaranth (*Gomphrena globosa*)
Sunflower (*Helianthus annuus*)
Moonflower (*Ipomoea alba*)
Nasturtium (*Nasturtium* spp.)
Marigolds (*Tagetes* spp.)
Zinnia (*Zinnia* spp.)

EASY ANNUALS FOR ALL-SEASON BLOOM

The best-known annuals are those that tend to bloom and bloom and bloom, regardless of hardballs thrown by weather, disease, and other natural disasters. Like a well-known boxer that keeps winning despite the number of years under his belt, these plants can roll with the punches and still maintain a sunny disposition. Start with high-performance cultivars ideal for your climate and remove faded blossoms to keep these annuals performing like champs.

> Ageratum (*Ageratum Houstonianum*)
> Wax begonia (*Begonia × semperflorens-cultorum*)
> Vinca (*Catharanthus roseus*)
> Flamingo Feather cockscomb (*Celosia cristata* 'Flamingo Feather')
>   Needs no deadheading
> Globe amaranth (*Gomphrena* spp.)
> New Guinea impatiens (*Impatiens* hyb.)
> Impatiens (*Impatiens Wallerana*)
> Spreading petunia (*Petunia* 'Purple Wave' and 'Pink Wave')
> Classic zinnia (*Zinnia angustifolia*)

LONG BLOOMERS WITH REJUVENATION

Some annuals need a little more care than others to provide a long season of bloom. The time spent in deadheading, cutting back lanky stems, fertilizing, and rejuvenating will be well rewarded with fresh new blooms.

> Spider flower (*Cleome Hasslerana*)
> China pinks (*Dianthus chinensis*)
> Geraniums (*Pelargonium × hortorum*)
> Grandiflora petunias (*Petunia × hybrida*)
> Scarlet sage (*Salvia splendens*)
> Marigold (*Tagetes* spp.)
> Pansy (*Viola × Wittrockiana*)

SHORT-TERM BLOOMERS

In a lifecycle that superficially mimics spring flowering bulbs, some annuals flower then fade away, sometimes leaving their mature seeds to bring about a new generation the following year.

> Cornflowers (*Centaurea Cyanus*)
> Baby's breath (*Gypsophila elegans*)
> Sunflowers (*Helianthus* spp.)
> Shirley poppies (*Papaver Rhoeas*)

WEATHER-PROOF ANNUALS COURTESY OF NONA WOLFRAM-KOIVULA

Sometimes the best annuals are those that won't fail come inclement weather. When rain starts pounding down hard and heat and humidity rise, some annuals may shatter, smash, wither, or fade away. But the following annuals can take everything nature throws at them and more, says Nona Wolfram-Koivula, executive director of All America Selections, a program that gives awards to exceptional new cultivars.

Fibrous rooted begonia (*Begonia sempervirens*)
Cockscomb (*Celosia plumosa* and *C. cristata*)
Impatiens (*Impatiens Wallerana*)
Multiflora petunias (*Petunia × hybrida*)
Floribunda petunias (*Petunia × hybrida*)
Mealycup salvia (*Salvia farinacea*)
Classic zinnia (*Zinnia angustifolia*)

BEWARE LIMITED FLOWER COLOR
"Melampodium is a wonderful plant and very heat tolerant, but the number of little gold flowers per plant have always disappointed me."
Nona Wolfram-Koivula, executive director of All America Selections, Downers Grove, Illinois

JIM NAU ON NEW ANNUAL CULTIVARS

Managing varieties for Ball Seed Company, one of America's largest annual seed wholesalers located in West Chicago, Illinois, Jim Nau keeps in touch with the newest and best annuals. He's particularly pleased with a new line of vegetatively propagated annuals collectively called Proven Winners. They include some of the following less common flowers.

Marguerite (*Chrysanthemum frutescens* 'Butterfly', 'Sugar Baby',
    'Summer Angel', and other in the Cobbitty Daisy series)
Bacopa (*Bacopa sutera cordata* 'Snowstorm' and 'Snowflake')
Goldie (*Bidens ferulifolia* 'Goldie')
Golden Beauty strawflower (*Helichrysum bracteatum* 'Golden Beauty')
Scaevola (*Scaevola aemula* 'New Wonder')

"Linaria 'Fantasy' is one new annual that does beautifully in the cool growing season but tends to fall apart in heat. It has beautiful vibrant colors and is ideal in mixed containers for spring or fall. Keep a potted linaria on the front step of house or back deck or patio where people can really take a good look at it. When the linaria fades in summer, it can be removed and replaced with something else like basil or cilantro."
Jim Nau, varieties manager for Ball Seed Company, West Chicago, Illinois

NATIVE CARNIVOROUS PLANTS

Some of the most startling plants are wetland natives that capture and consume insects for their nitrogen. Although some are perennials, they also can be grown as annuals in a basin of distilled water outdoors beneath a tree. My children routinely pick up one or more carnivorous plants each spring, and we keep them on the kitchen window sill where they catch their share of flies and always provoke conversation.

Venus fly trap (*Dionaea muscipula*)
Sundews (*Drosera* spp.)
Pitcher plant (*Sarracenia* spp.)

Pitcher
Plant

Annuals in the Landscape

Annuals fit cheerfully into many landscape niches—containers, fragrance gardens, and cutting, theme, and all-purpose gardens. Although the classic impatiens and geraniums can make outstanding displays, more uncommon but delightful annuals like verbenas and stock add variety and bragging rights. Greenhouses offering a large selection of plants or specialists in unusual plants are likely to carry less common annuals. They also can be started from seed available from mail-order catalogs.

FRAGRANT ANNUALS

Some highly bred annuals come in such novel shapes, colors, and configurations that Mother Nature would hardly recognize her creations. In the breeding process, fragrance may be sacrificed along the way. For a fragrant garden, old-fashioned flowers can be the best.

Sweet William (*Dianthus barbatus*)
Moonflower (*Ipomoea alba*)
Sweet pea (*Lathyrus odoratus*)
Sweet alyssum (*Lobularia maritima*)
Stock (*Matthiola incana*)
Four-o'clock (*Mirabilis Jalapa*)
Domino Hybrid flowering tobacco (*Nicotiana alata* 'Domino Hybrids')
Candelabra flowering tobacco (*Nicotiana sylvestris*)
Mignonette (*Reseda odorata* 'Fragrant Beauty')
Signet marigolds (*Tagetes signata*)

SEEDS FOR BIRD FOOD

By allowing annual flowers to go to seed at the end of the growing season, you can observe a fine crop of small birds such as chickadees, titmice, and goldfinches. As a bonus, some annuals also may return from self-sown seed next year.

Calliopsis (*Coreopsis tinctoria*)
Cosmos (*Cosmos* spp.)
Blanket flower (*Gaillardia pulchella*)

Sunflower (*Helianthus annuus*)
Marigolds (*Tagetes* spp.)
Zinnia (*Zinnia elegans*)

"Cantigny visitors are particularly interested in the identities of new plants, especially if they're colorful. But finding those same plants at commercial greenhouses can be challenging. We've found that about 10 to 20 percent of the greenhouses around here carry them."
Joe Sable, horticulturist for Cantigny Gardens in Wheaton, Illinois

JOE SABLE'S FAVORITE UNUSUAL ANNUALS

As horticulturist for Cantigny Gardens, an estate-turned-park in Wheaton, Illinois, Joe Sable has years of experimentation with annuals under his belt. The Cantigny formal gardens are famous for their annual displays, which can include 100,000 annuals of up to 500 different varieties. Many are set in geometric beds amid arching walkways and hedges and beside ponds and arbors. Some of the most outstandingly unusual annuals include the following.

Butterfly Yellow chrysanthemum (*Chrysanthemum frutescens* 'Butterfly Yellow')
Basil (*Ocimum Basilicum* 'Purple Ruffles')
Black-eyed Susan (*Rudbeckia hirta* 'Indian Summer')
Coleus (*Coleus* × *hybridus* 'Belingrath', 'Alabama', 'Burgundy Flame', 'Cantigny Royale', 'Gay's Delight', 'Rustic Orange', 'Saturn', and 'Pistachio Cantigny Royale')
Dahlberg daisy (*Dyssodia tenuiloba*)
Goldmarie fern-leaved beggar-ticks (*Bidens ferulifolia* 'Goldmarie')
Mermaid Blue lisianthus (*Eustoma grandiflorum* 'Mermaid Blue')
Daybreak gazania (*Gazania rigens* 'Daybreak Mix')
Strawberry Fields globe amaranth (*Gomphrena globosa* 'Strawberry Fields')
Sweet potato (*Ipomoea Batatas* 'Little Blackie', 'Sulphur', and 'Tricolor')
Stargazer blue star (*Laurentia axillaris* 'Stargazer')
Miniature hollyhock (*Lavatera trimestris*)
Sparkler star of the veldt (*Osteospermum* 'Sparkler')
Fountain grass (*Pennisetum setaceum*)
Purple Wave petunia (*Petunia* spp. 'Purple Wave')
Verbena (*Verbena bonariensis*)
Zinnia (*Zinnia angustifolia* 'Crystal White')

Cantigny Gardens has been made famous by the coleus 'Cantigny Royale' that bears its name. A muddy brown colored 'Duck's Foot' coleus growing in the Cantigny greenhouse sported a handsome violet-leaved stem, which was made into a cutting, grown on, and now is sold through some local nurseries and national mail order catalogs.

The deep burgundy to nearly black foliage has chartreuse along the leaf margins and makes a dynamic display when planted with silver-leaved dusty miller or white flowers. With small, duck-foot shaped leaves, it grows into a neat mound shape, is unlikely to flower and change its form, and tolerates summer heat and full sun rather well.

ANNUALS FOR CUTTING

Any annual is suitable for cutting and setting in a vase. But the best of the cut flowers will stay fresh for at least several days. When wanted for a large vase or tall arrangement, look for sturdy, long-stemmed cultivars—not just any bedding annual will do. (Some sunflowers will shed messy pollen unless you start with cultivars that are pollen free.) Use this list as a beginning then add your own favorite cut flowers.

Blue Horizon ageratum (*Ageratum Houstonianum* 'Blue Horizon')
White dill (*Ammi majus*)
Rocket snapdragon (*Antirrhinum majus* 'Rocket')
Burpleurum (*Burpleurum Griffithii*)
Prince pot marigold (*Calendula officinalis* 'Prince')
China asters, long stemmed (*Callistephus chinensis* 'Super Giants'
      and 'Bouquet Powderpuffs')
Cockscomb, long stemmed (*Celosia cristata* 'Chief' or 'Flamingo Feather')
Cornflower, long stemmed (*Centaurea Cyanus* 'Florist Blue Boy')
Larkspur (*Delphinium Consolida*)
Baby's breath (*Gypsophila elegans*)
Cutting sunflowers (*Helianthus annuus* and H. *debilis*)
Hybrid sunflowers, pollen free (*Helianthus hybridus* 'Sunrich Lemon',
      'Sunrich Orange', 'Sunbeam')
Heliotrope (*Heliotrope arborescens* 'Marine')
Sweet pea (*Lathyrus odoratus*)
Lavatera (*Lavatera trimestris*)
Bells of Ireland (*Moluccella laevis*)
Gloriosa daisy (*Rudbeckia hirta*)
Mealycup salvia (*Salvia farinacea*)
Zinnia (*Z. elegans* 'State Fair Mix', 'Ruffles Mix')

EVERLASTING FLOWERS

Flowers often are thought to be the most delicate of creations, but the blossoms on these annuals are just the opposite. Their petals are tissue- or strawlike and are easily air-dried for arrangements or wreaths. People who complain that the gardening season is too short in the Midwest will particularly enjoy everlastings that can be used around the house long after the garden shuts down.

Winged everlasting (*Ammobium alatum*)
Quaking grass (*Briza maxima*)
Flamingo Feather cockscomb (*Celosia spicata*)
Globe amaranth (*Gomphrena globosa*)
Strawflowers (*Helichrysum* spp.)
Sunrays (*Helipterum roseum*)
Statice (*Limonium sinensis*)
Russian statice (*Limonium Suworowii*)
Golden ageratum (*Lonas annua*)
Love-in-a-mist pods (*Nigella damascena*)
Star flower (*Scabiosa stellata*)
Immortelles (*Xeranthemum annuum*)

BEYOND BEDDING

Most of the annuals you'll see in a Midwestern garden center are low growing, developed to spread into a colorful carpet. But some taller annuals can be spectacular additions to the garden too. They can fill rear ranks (or the center of an island bed) and make colorful transitions between shrubs and perennials.

Blue Horizon ageratum (*Ageratum Houstonianum* 'Blue Horizon')
Prince pot marigold (*Calendula officinalis* 'Prince')
Cosmos (*Cosmos* spp.)
Cockscomb (*Celosia cristata* 'Chief'; *C. spicata* 'Flamingo Feather')
Spider flower (*Cleome Hasslerana*)
Heliotrope (*Heliotrope arborescens* 'Marine')
Lavatera (*Lavatera trimestris*)
Flowering tobacco (*Nicotiana alata* 'Lumina')
Gloriosa daisy (*Rudbeckia hirta*)
Mealycup salvia (*Salvia farinacea*)
Jubilee American marigold (*Tagetes erecta* 'Jubilee')

ANNUALS THAT ATTRACT WILDLIFE

Some annual flowers have more than just a pretty face. Their nectar can nourish hummingbirds or butterflies and their seeds feed browsing birds.

HUMMINGBIRD ANNUALS

With a long season of bloom, these annuals can keep hummingbirds coming back most of the summer and into fall.

Spider flower (*Cleome Hasslerana*)
Cardinal climber (*Ipomoea multifida*)
Crimson Rambler morning glory (*Ipomoea tricolor* 'Crimson Rambler')
Flowering tobacco (*Nicotiana alata*)
Petunia, red and pink (*Petunia × hybrida*)
Phlox, Drummond (*Phlox Drummondii*)
Scarlet sage (*Salvia splendens*)
Texas sage (*Salvia coccinea*)
Nasturtium (*Tropaeolum majus*)

BUTTERFLY ANNUALS

Calendula (*Calendula officinalis*)
Spider flower (*Cleome spinosa*)
Cosmos (*Cosmos sulphureus*)
Sunflowers (*Helianthus annuus*)
Impatiens (*Impatiens Wallerana*)
Lantana (*Lantana* hyb.)
Pincushion flower (*Scabiosa atropurpurea*)
Verbena (*Verbena* spp.)
Zinnia (*Zinnia* spp.)

PAM DUTHIE'S FAVORITE ANNUALS OF A PERENNIAL LOVER

A perennial garden specialist with a Chicago-area landscape design business, teacher and lecturer Pam Duthie looks at annuals as supplemental to perennials and uses them as accents for texture or flower color. She particularly likes annuals like larkspur that reseed themselves or *perennialize* and come back year after year. (They are marked with an asterisk.)

FLOWERING ANNUALS
*Spider flower (*Cleome Hassleriana*)
*Larkspur (*Consolida ambigua*)
Compact white cosmos (*Cosmos bipinnatus* 'Sonata')
China pinks (*Dianthus chinensis*)
Bizzy lizzie (*Impatiens Wallerana*), Only for accents not perennial garden edgers
Blue stars (*Laurentia axilaris*)
Blue lobelia (*Lobelia Erinus* 'Sapphire')
*Sweet alyssum (*Lobularia maritima*)
Baby blue eyes (*Nemophila Menziesii*)
Chartreuse flowering tobacco (*Nicotiana Langsdorfii*)
Love-in-a-mist (*Nigella damascena*)
Victoria blue salvia (*Salvia farinacea* 'Victoria')
Blue Wonder fan flower (*Scaevola aemula* 'Blue Wonder')
*Tall verbena (*Verbena bonariensis*)
Imagination creeping verbena (*Verbena* 'Imagination')
Pansy (*Viola × Wittrockiana*)
White compact zinnia (*Zinnia angustifolia* 'Tropical Snow')

ANNUALS FOR FOLIAGE
Burgundy coleus (*Coleus Blumei*)
Chartreuse coleus (*Coleus* 'Golden Bedder')
Variegated licorice plant (*Helichrysum petiolatum* 'Variegata')
Blackie sweet potato (*Ipomoea* 'Blackie')
*Chinese basil (*Perilla frutescens* 'Purpurea')

Burgundy
Coleus

"Annuals act as season-bridgers when interplanted in the perennial garden, but beware of annuals like geraniums, marigolds, and dahlias that become huge and shade out newly planted perennials."
Pam Duthie, lecturer and owner of the Gifted Gardener in Chicago, Illinois

ANNUALS WITH COLORFUL FOLIAGE

Not one to miss the forest for the trees, I would be remiss not to mention annuals with colorful foliage. Some begonias have subtle burgundy-colored leaves best highlighted beside brighter greens or silvers. New Guinea impatiens and coleus, with variegated white, pink, and green leaves, are bold color accents, especially when topped by vivid flowers.

Joseph's coat (*Amaranthus tricolor* 'Joseph's Coat')
Begonias, burgundy leaf (*Begonia sempervirens* 'Gin',
    'Brandy', 'Rum', 'Vodka', and 'Whiskey')
Flowering kale and cabbage (*Brassica oleracea*)
Wine Sparkler cockscomb (*Celosia globosa*
    'Wine Sparkler')
Coleus (*Coleus* spp.)
Kochia (*Kochia scoparia*)
Castor bean (*Ricinus communis*)
Dusty miller (*Senecio Cineraria*)

Castor
Bean

DIANE WHEALY'S FAVORITE HEIRLOOM ANNUALS

Heirloom plants are the stock in trade at Heritage Farm near Decorah, Iowa. This is where Diane Whealy, co-founder of the Seed Saver's Exchange, does her share to propagate and preserve species from yesteryear. She is especially interested in old-fashioned annuals (and a few token biennials that bloom the second year after planting), such as those below.

'Outhouse' hollyhock (*Alcea rosea*)
    A 9-foot tall biennial with single white, pink, magenta, and dark burgundy
      flowers
Sweet William (*Dianthus barbatus*)
    Biennial of mixed colors to 1½ feet
'Glittering Prizes' foxglove (*Digitalis purpurea*)
    Spotted white and pink bells on 6-foot tall stalks; biennial and self-seeding
'Grandpa Ott's' morning glory (*Ipomoea* spp.)
    Purple flower with red-starred throat
Old-fashioned vining petunia (*Petunia* spp.)
    2- to 3-foot stems with fragrant mixed white, lavender, and purple flowers
Kiss me over the garden gate (*Polygonum orientale*)
    Self-seeding annual 6- to 9-feet tall with pendulous, dark pink catkins

> **"'Grandpa Ott's' morning glories were brought by my grandfather's father from Bulgaria to America. We've been pleased to find they grow well throughout the Midwest. Before the time of indoor plumbing, 'Outhouse' hollyhocks were planted around outhouses so that women visitors wouldn't have to be embarrassed by asking where the outhouse was. They could just look for the flowers."**
> **Diane Whealy, Seed Saver's Exchange, Decorah, Iowa**

ORNAMENTAL GRASSES FOR CONTAINERS FROM MICHELLE D'ARCY

Ornamental grasses and flowering annuals can make particularly spectacular companions for large pots or planters. Michelle D'Arcy, with Horticultural Associates, Inc., regularly combines both for her Chicago-area customers. Here are some of the most successful grasses; Michelle's absolute favorites are marked with an asterisk.

*Quaking grass (*Briza media*)
*Karl Foerster feather reed grass (*Calamagrostis arundinacea* 'Karl Foerster')
*Golden variegated Japanese sedge (*Carex Morrowii* 'Goldband')
*Blue wild rye (*Leymus arenarius* 'Glaucus')
Blue fescue (*Festuca glauca*)
Golden variegated hakonechloa (*Hakonechloa macra* 'Aureola')
Blue oat grass (*Helictotrichon sempervirens*)
Japanese blood grass (*Imperata cylindrica* 'Red Baron')
Maiden grass (*Miscanthus sinensis* 'Gracillimus')
Silver variegated maiden grass (*Miscanthus sinensis* 'Morning Light')
Silver Feather variegated maiden grass (*Miscanthus sinensis* 'Silberfeder')
Nippon maiden grass (*Miscanthus sinensis* 'Nippon')
*Yaku Jima maiden grass (*Miscanthus sinensis* 'Yaku Jima')
*Fountain grass (*Pennisetum alopecuroides*)
Dwarf fountain grass (*Pennisetum alopecuroides* 'Hamelyn')
Little Bunny fountain grass (*Pennisetum alopecuroides* 'Little Bunny')
Oriental fountain grass (*Pennisetum orientale*)
*Ribbon grass (*Phalaris arundinacea*)

"I've been using grasses more and more in large containers where they are fantastic planted with roses, annuals, herbs, or perennials. The grasses can be discarded at the end of the season like annuals or I've had some success transplanting them into a garden bed for the winter."
Michelle D'Arcy, Horticultural Associates, Inc., Gurnee, Illinois

ANNUALS FOR HANGING BASKETS

For hanging pots and baskets dripping with color, you need cascading annuals. Their airy beauty is the perfect focal point for deck, patio, or porch.

Tuberous begonias (*Begonia* × *tuberhybrida*)
Vinca (*Catharanthus roseus*)
Coleus (*Coleus* spp.)
Fuchsia (*Fuchsia* spp.)
Lobelia (*Lobelia Erinus*)

Geraniums, ivy (*Pelargonium peltatum*)
Petunias (*Petunia* × *hybrida*)
Imagination verbena (*Verbena* × *hybrida* 'Imagination')
Vinca vine (*Vinca major*)

TROPICALS FOR CONTAINERS
　　One way to give a verdant, lush appearance to annual pots and baskets is to interplant tropical foliage plants with annual flowers. Dracaenas, Boston ferns, caladiums, Chinese evergreens, and crotons add interesting texture and color amid the flowers.

VINES

Tarzan, the only hero I know who uses vines for transportation, makes the most of tropical lianas—broad-leaved philodendrons, glorious bougainvilleas, exotic vanilla orchids, and sturdier swinging type vines draping amid tree canopies. But vines are also useful closer to home where their climbing and clinging luxuriance gives a nearly tropical effect to the Midwestern garden. In my own yard, wild grape vines weave through the lattice-work below my deck, and Virginia creeper clothes tree trunks in nearby woodlands. Gifts from nature, vines color and disguise otherwise barren structures throughout the growing season. In your yard, trellised vines might be put to work blocking out unsightly views or hiding utility boxes, air conditioners, and the like.

Compared with trees, shrubs, and perennials, there is a limited selection of vines well suited for the Midwest. One or two will be all most properties need. Because certain ground covers and roses may also behave as vining plants, see the chapters on ground covers and roses for more ideas.

Right Plant, Right Place

Vines have special qualities above and beyond ordinary plants, which influence where you can use them. How they climb, the lengths they go to, and their hardiness are particularly important. As with the rest of the plant kingdom, it's vital to put a vine in the right site and soil.

 Vines that become dense or woody, like the climbing hydrangea, need sturdy supports that can bear increasing weight for the lifetime of the vine. Don't be tempted by the flimsy plastic trellises available at some discount stores. Build a sturdy wooden framework instead.

MATCHING CLIMBING STYLES TO SUPPORTS

Vines use differing strategies to rise above the rest. Vines like wisteria encircle upright objects and shimmy up them. Grape vines (*Vitis* spp.) grasp supports with tendrils or small stems and pull their way up. Clematis (*Clematis* spp.) both twines and loops its leaves over supports, a two-pronged climbing strategy. English ivy (*Hedera* spp.) and Virginia creeper (*Parthenocissus quinquefolia*) have suction-cuplike appendages that allow them to stick to walls or tree trunks. As clinging vines they can climb solid objects, walls, and posts unaided.

CLINGERS

These athletic climbers have suction-cuplike holdfasts and can scale nearly any solid object, wrapping it in greenery. Some of the hallowed Georgian halls of my alma matter, Miami University in Oxford, Ohio, were draped romantically in a bit of ivy, but not everyone wants it climbing all over their house. Although the holdfasts don't cause structural damage, they can remove paint. The weight of the vines may dislodge windowsills or weak ledges. If concerned, keep clingers away from the house or plan to do some serious pruning when climbing commences.

Wintercreeper (*Euonymus Fortunei*)
Ivy (*Hedera* spp.)
Climbing hydrangea (*Hydrangea anomala* subsp. *petiolaris*)
Virginia creeper (*Parthenocissus quinquefolia*)
Boston ivy (*Parthenocissus tricuspidata*)

Boston Ivy

TWINERS

These vines are ideal for planting beside poles, fence posts, trellises, and arbors because they will encircle any moderately narrow post or lathwork. Some may even wind around themselves if unable to find other supports. A little guidance by hand will help prevent rat's nests of tangled stems.

Hardy kiwi (*Actinidia arguta*)
Kolomikta vine (*Actinidia Kolomikta*)
Akebia (*Akebia* spp.)
Dutchman's pipe (*Aristolochia durior*)
Bittersweet (*Celastrus* spp.)
Clematis (*Clematis* spp.)
Common hop (*Humulus Lupulus*)
Morning glories (*Ipomoea* spp.)
Scarlet runner bean (*Phaseolus coccineus*)
Silver lace vine (*Polygonum Aubertii*)
Wisteria (*Wisteria* spp.)

TENDRILS

Trellises, arbors, and chain-link and open-weave fences lend themselves to this type of vine. Grapes will climb about anything they can get their tendrils on and compact clematis are marvelous creeping up the barren bases of roses or other bare-bottomed shrubs.

Porcelain berry (*Ampelopsis* spp.)
Clematis, some (*Clematis* spp.)
Sweet pea (*Lathyrus odoratus*)
Loofah gourd (*Luffa aegyptiaca*)
Grapes (*Vitis* spp.)

PETER VAN DER LINDEN ON LESS COMMON VINES IN THE MORTON ARBORETUM COLLECTIONS

Over seventy species of vines, many native to America, grow on arbors across the Morton Arboretum grounds in Lisle, Illinois. Peter van der Linden, Morton Arboretum curator of plant collections, recommended some of his favorites, vines graced with ornamental qualities yet seldom troubled with problems and unlikely to escape and take over nearby plantings.

Note: One outstanding new Chinese clematis called *Clematis intricata* or *C. glauca* is not included on this list because it is not available commercially. But with lovely gray-green leaves, yellow flowers borne intermittently over the summer, and fluffy seed heads that persist all winter, it's one to watch for in the future.

Grape honeysuckle (*Lonicera prolifera*)
*Silk vine (*Periploca sepium*)
Magnolia vine (*Schisandra chinensis*)
Bay star vine (*Schisandra glabra*)
Kentucky wisteria (*Wisteria macrostachya*)
American wisteria (*Wisteria frutescens*)

*Note: Silk vine can spread into nearby plantings but doesn't self-sow.

"Clematis species can't be growing together on a trellis or they can crowd each other out. We've even found several clematis species, namely the Italian clematis (*Clematis Viticella*) and *C. serratifolia*, that were so aggressive that they would move to neighboring trellises and begin smothering those vines. We've stopped growing *C. serratifolia* in our collections as a consequence.

"Kiwi vines including Taro vine (*Actinidia arguta*), *A. Kolomikta*, and silver vine (*A. polygama*) do well here. They are somewhat drought sensitive and *A. Kolomikta* has occasional Japanese beetle damage, but overall, they work well.

"I have been disappointed by the porcelain berry (*Ampelopsis brevipedunculata*). I had high expectations after reading glowing reports but here the fruit is not produced in large enough quantities to justify its reputation."

Peter van der Linden, curator of plant collections at Morton Arboretum, Lisle, Illinois

JOE OPPE'S CLASSIC DES MOINES VINES

Although the soil is rich and loose in the heartland of Iowa, summer is sweltering and winter lows can drop to -30 degrees F. Gardeners in Des Moines tend to have a conservative nature, using the following sturdy growers they've seen time and time again and know will succeed.

Trumpet creeper (*Campsis radicans*)
Red anemone clematis (*Clematis montana* var. *rubens*)
American bittersweet (*Celastrus scandens*)
Golden European hop (*Humulus Lupulus* 'Aureus')
Goldflame honeysuckle (*Lonicera × Heckrottii*)
Silver fleece vine (*Polygonum Aubertii*)
Frost grape (*Vitis vulpina*)

"Des Moines has days and days of dry weather. To keep plants from drying up, you have to use tons and tons of mulch, which has made me become more mulch focused here than anywhere."
Joe Oppe, horticulturist for Des Moines Botanical Garden

VINES THAT DO WELL IN POOR, DRY SOIL

Vines that will grow in dry, barren areas—on a droughty bank, rock pile, or perimeter of the yard out of hose-reach—may be hard to get rid of elsewhere, but in this case, they can be just what the doctor ordered.

American bittersweet (*Celastrus scandens*)
Hall's Japanese honeysuckle (*Lonicera japonica* 'Halliana')
Silver lace vine (*Polygonum Aubertii*)

VINES FEARED FOR THEIR VIGOR

Although homeowners may delight in their woodland garden carpeted with evergreen ivy, just ask a botanist for an opinion of the plant and you'll be in for an eye opening experience. Vigorous vines like ivy, grapes, and a number of others can grow so aggressively that they consume a garden, escape into nearby wildlands, meadows, and thickets and squeeze out the rightful occupants. Use the following with care; their vigor means you must keep your pruning shears sharpened. (Other vines may also qualify for this list if given ideal growing conditions.)

Porcelain berry (*Ampelopsis brevipedunculata*)
Chinese bittersweet (*Celastrus orbiculatus*)
English ivy (*Hedera helix*)
Japanese honeysuckle (*Lonicera japonica*)
Virginia creeper (*Parthenocissus quinquefolia*)
Boston ivy (*Parthenocissus tricuspidata*)
Silver lace vine (*Polygonum Aubertii*)
Wisteria (*Wisteria* spp.)

EXCELLENT CELMATIS FROM CHICAGO BOTANIC GARDEN TRIALS

Trials of sixty-four clematis species and varieties were conducted at Chicago Botanic Garden from 1990 to 1995. Vines were planted in clay loam soils with varying sun exposures, given minimal maintenance, mulch, and a 12- to 18-inch high cage to prevent rabbit damage. With the exception of early-flowering species, vines were pruned in late winter to remove dead stems and keep the vines within their allotted space. The best cultivars and species proved superior in many ways: flower color, size, bloom period, and overall coverage, plant height and form, pest and disease resistance, healthiness, winter hardiness, and adaptability. Nine of the sixty-four were considered superior performers.

'Bees Jubilee'
'Comtesse de Bouchaud'
Durand clematis (*Clematis* × *Durandii*)
Praecox clematis (*Clematis* × *Jouiniana* 'Praecox')
Macropetala clematis (*Clematis macropetala*)
'Ville de Lyon'
Italian clematis (*Clematis Viticella* 'Etoile Violette', and
    'Grandiflora Sanguinea')
'Vyvyan Pennell'

Over half of the tested clematis in the Chicago Botanic Garden trials rated good to excellent, showing great promise for Midwestern landscapes. But for best results in your yard, consider the following advice.

"[T]he best results were seen in south-facing positions. . . . Providing shade for the base of the plant helped moderate the soil temperature and retain the necessary soil moisture. Too much competition limited the growth of some plants, but most clematis mixed well with their companions and usually held their own in the garden."

Richard Hawke, from Plant Evaluation Notes, *Chicago Botanic Garden, Issue 10, 1997*

VINES LESS ATTRACTIVE TO DEER

A rapidly growing silver lace vine might be a match for the appetite of a hungry deer but if one of these greedy herbivores severs the lower stem the contest is over. If deer are dominant around your domicile, plant vines they are not known to enjoy.

Akebia (*Akebia* spp.)
Trumpet vine (*Campsis* spp.)
Bittersweet (*Celastrus* spp.)
Clematis (*Clematis* spp.)
Climbing hydrangea (*Hydrangea anomala* subsp. *petiolaris*)
Honeysuckle (*Lonicera* spp.)
Virginia creeper (*Parthenocissus quinquefolia*)
Boston ivy (*Parthenocissus tricuspidata*)
Wisteria (*Wisteria* spp.)

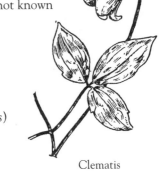

Clematis

VINES FOR SHADE

Only a few vines do extremely well in the shade. Vines with variegated leaves may revert to all-green if grown in the shade. For evergreens such as English ivy and winter creeper, winter shade can help prevent sun scorching.

English ivy (*Hedera helix*)
Winter creeper (*Euonymus Fortunei*)
Climbing hydrangea (*Hydrangea petiolaris*)

VINES THAT WILL GROW IN SUN OR PARTIAL SHADE

Five-leaf akebia (*Akebia quinata*)
Dutchman's pipe (*Aristolochia durior*)
Trumpetcreeper (*Campsis radicans*)
Wintercreeper (*Euonymus Fortunei*)
Climbing hydrangea (*Hydrangea anomala* subsp. *petiolaris*)
Japanese honeysuckle (*Lonicera japonica*)
Trumpet honeysuckle (*Lonicera sempervirens*)
Boston ivy (*Parthenocissus tricuspidata*)
Virginia creeper (*Parthenocissus quinquefolia*)
Silver lace vine (*Polygonum Aubertii*)

Trumpet Honeysuckle

VINES THAT REACH A LONG, LONG WAY

Unlike perennials and shrubs that max out at a certain height, some vines can keep growing and growing. They may be perfect for roofing a big structure, like the angled outdoor reading room beneath a pergola at the Cleveland Botanical Garden or for covering an arbor or scaling a big oak tree. But their vigor can get out of hand, so beware and be ready to prune. The following approximate lengths will give you an idea of what you'll be dealing with.

50 FEET OR LONGER

Virginia creeper (*Parthenocissus quinquefolia*)
Boston ivy (*Parthenocissus tricuspidata*)
Climbing hydrangea (*Hydrangea anomala* subsp. *petiolaris*)

30 TO 40 FEET

Hardy kiwi (*Actinidia arguta*)
Trumpet creeper (*Campsis radicans*)
Trumpet honeysuckle (*Lonicera sempervirens*)
Silver lace vine (*Polygonum Aubertii*)
Wisteria (*Wisteria* spp.)

20 TO 30 FEET

Five-leaf akebia (*Akebia quinata*)
Porcelain berry (*Ampelopsis brevipedunculata*)
Dutchman's pipe (*Aristolochia durior*)
Japanese honeysuckle (*Lonicera japonica*)

15 TO 20 FEET
>Kolomikta vine (*Actinidia Kolomikta*)
>Jackman clematis (*Clematis Jackmanii*)

Vines through the Seasons

Today as I write, the mercury tops 95 degrees and the pavement sends up steam after a brief thundershower—summer is hanging heavy. But summer is rich with flowering clematis, scarlet runner beans, and vining nasturtiums. Come autumn, the fruits of bittersweet and porcelain berry will make a dynamic last splash before winter. In the winter, there will be the exfoliating bark of a mature climbing hydrangea vine and the fluffy seed heads of clematis. As spring progresses, the air is warmed with the fragrance of sweet peas. Plan ahead for a year of pleasant surprises from your vines.

A SAMPLER OF BLOOMS BY SEASON

Color coordinate your vines with your other flowers and flowering trees and shrubs for a tailored harmony. Here are some samples of approximate flowering times for different vines.

SPRING-BLOOMING VINES
>Spring blooming clematis (*Clematis* spp. including *lanuginosa* group)
>Sweet pea (*Lathyrus odoratus*)
>Winter honeysuckle (*Lonicera fragrantissima*)
>Goldflame honeysuckle (*Lonicera* × *Heckrottii*)
>Trumpet honeysuckle (*Lonicera sempervirens*)
>Wisteria (*Wisteria* spp.)

SUMMER-BLOOMING VINES
>Trumpet creeper (*Campsis radicans*)
>Summer blooming clematis (*Clematis* spp. including × *Jackmanii*)
>Sweet autumn clematis (*Clematis maximowicziana*)
>Anemone clematis (*Clematis montana*)
>Climbing hydrangea (*Hydrangea anomala* subsp. *petiolaris*)
>Moonflower (*Ipomoea alba*)
>Japanese honeysuckle (*Lonicera japonica*)
>Scarlet runner vine (*Phaseolus coccineus*)
>Silver lace vine (*Polygonum Aubertii*)
>Vining nasturtium (*Tropaeolum majus*)

FALL-BLOOMING VINES
>Sweet autumn clematis (*Clematis maximowicziana*)
>Moonflower (*Ipomoea alba*)
>Sweet pea (*Lathyrus odoratus*)
>Vining nasturtium (*Tropaeolum majus*)

The arts often reflect the beauty of the seasons with dynamic vividness. This is particularly true of the Ohara School of Ikebana (Japanese flower arrangement). Differing from western arrangements and growing in popularity in America, the Ohara School uses flowers and foliage to depict landscapes through the seasons, making cut flowers live again through precise placement and sensitivity.

"The seasons are the basis of this form of Ikebana, which keeps me constantly in harmony with nature. As nature changes, the arranger changes too. The plant material varies early, middle, and late in each season, and that radically influences what you can do with it. Vines, for example, make me think of fall, hanging arrangements full of fruits. You don't regret the passing of one season because you are looking forward to the next. It's the cycle of life that you can feel in yourself."

Ingrid Luders, First Master Degree, Sub-Grand Master of the Ohara School of Ikebana, Cleveland, Ohio

VINES WITH INTERESTING LEAF COLORS

Some vines have colorful foliage throughout the growing season, and in the case of evergreen vines, deep into winter.

Kolkitia actinidia (*Actinidia Kolomikta*)
Silver Dust English ivy (*Hedera helix* 'Silverdust')
Gold netted Japanese honeysuckle (*Lonicera japonica* 'Aureo-reticulata')
Purple Japanese honeysuckle (*Lonicera japonica* var. *purpurea*)
Purple Boston ivy (*Parthenocissus tricuspidata* 'Purpurea')

HARDY EVERGREEN VINES

Although it can be hard to do in the middle of summer, think winter for a moment. By planning ahead, you can blend evergreen trees, shrubs, vines, and ground covers so you'll never mourn for lack of green vegetation. Here are some evergreen vines to include in the mix.

Five leaf akebia (*Akebia quinata*) Semi-evergreen; drops leaves in winter
English ivy (*Hedera helix*)
Japanese honeysuckle (*Lonicera japonica*)
Wintercreeper (*Euonymus Fortunei*)

CLEMATIS ACCORDING TO PRUNING NEEDS

Many Midwestern gardeners have a passion for clematis, that queen of vines with showy flowers produced at many different times during the growing season. Different species and hybrids may bloom in spring, summer, or fall; some flower several times a year. These clematis can require different pruning schemes to shape and rejuvenate vines without removing all-important flower buds. These timing lists are approximate; consult your Cooperative Extension Service agent to learn the extent of pruning needed by different species and cultivars.

PRUNE IN EARLY SPRING FOR SUMMER BLOOM

'Comtesse de Bouchard'
'Duchess of Albany'
'Duchess of Sutherland'
'Ernest Markham'
'Gypsy Queen'
'Hagley Hybrid'
'Henryi'
'Lilacina Floribunda'
'Mrs. Robert Brydon'
'Niobe'
'Perle d'Azur'
'Pink Champagne'
'Venosa Violacea'
'Victoria'
'Ville de Lyon'
Alba Plena clematis (*Clematis florida* 'Alba Plena')
Sieboldii clematis (*Clematis florida* 'Sieboldii')
Jackman's clematis (*C.* × *Jackmanii*)
Candida clematis (*C. languinosa* 'Candida')
Sweet autumn clematis (*Clematis maximowicziana*)
Tangutica clematis (*Clematis Tangutica*)
Virgin's bower (*Clematis virginiana*)
Italian clematis (*Clematis Viticella*)
Purple Italian clematis (*Clematis Viticella* 'Purpurea Plena Elegans')

Virgin's
Bower

PRUNE AFTER FLOWERING FOR EARLY SEASON BLOOM

'Barbara Dibley'
'Barbara Jackman'
'Duchess of Edinburgh'
'Gillian Blades'
'Kathleen Dunford'
'Kathleen Wheeler'
'Lincoln Star'
'Marie Boisselot'
'The President'
Clematis patens

VINES WITH SHOWY FRUIT AND FALL COLOR

The following vines produce late-season berries or seed pods that can persist well into the autumn.

BLUE OR PURPLE FRUIT

Shiro Bana akebia (*Akebia quinata* 'Shiro Bana')
Porcelain berry (*Ampelopsis brevipedunculata*)
Virginia creeper (*Parthenocissus quinquefolia*)
Boston ivy (*Parthenocissus tricuspidata*)
Green Showers Boston ivy (*Parthenocissus tricuspidata* 'Green Showers')
Grapes (*Vitis* spp.)

Grapes

RED FRUIT

American bittersweet (*Celastrus scandens*) (Only on female plants with nearby males)
Wintercreeper (*Euonymus Fortunei*)
Trumpet honeysuckle (*Lonicera sempervirens*)
Berries Jubilee honeysuckle (*Lonicera Periclymenum* 'Berries Jubilee')
Grapes (*Vitis* spp.)

INTERESTING SEED PODS

Clematis, some (*Clematis* spp. including 'Bees Jubilee', *C. macropetala*, and *C. Viticella* 'Etoile Violette')
Scarlet runner beans (*Phaseolus coccineus*)
Wisteria (*Wisteria* spp.)

FALL COLOR

Bittersweet (*Celastrus* spp.)
Purple-leaf wintercreeper (*Euonymus Fortunei* 'Colorata')
Boston ivy (*Parthenocissus tricuspidata*)
Virginia creeper (*Parthenocissus quinquefolia*)

Vines in the Landscape

Let your fantasies carry you away when imagining what you can do with vines around your house. Then be prudent, and make sure your dream vines have appropriate colors, fragrances, coverage, and vigor.

VINES THAT MAKE GOOD GROUND COVER

If you set a vine free expecting it to grow up a nearby support, you may be in for a surprise. Some vines are as likely to grow outward as upward. One of the most beautiful ground hugging vines I've seen was at Gardenview Botanical Garden in Strongsville, Ohio, where director and gardener Henry Ross made a frothy blanket of white flowered virgin's bower clematis at the base of taller, barren-stemmed perennials. Here are some other vines that will do double duty.

Five-leaf akebia (*Akebia quinata*)
Durandii clematis (*Clematis × Durandii*)
Wintercreeper (*Euonymus Fortunei*)
English ivy (*Hedera helix*)
Japanese honeysuckle (*Lonicera japonica*)
Boston ivy (*Parthenocissus tricuspidata*)
Virginia creeper (*Parthenocissus quinquefolia*)

QUICK-CHANGE ANNUAL VINES

If you're the kind of person who likes to rearrange your living room on a regular basis, you'll probably enjoy growing annual vines. They give the garden a refreshing new look every year. All quick growers in warm weather, they can put on a nice display in a short period of time. When cold weather comes, they die and make it easy to plant something else. If allowed to set seed, morning glories and moonflowers, in particular, may arise from seedlings next summer and attempt to claim their previous space and more.

LAVISH GROWERS
Morning glory (*Convolvulus tricolor*)
Japanese hop (*Humulus japonicus*)
Moonflower (*Ipomoea alba*)
Red morning glory (*Ipomoea coccinea*)
Common morning glory (*Ipomoea purpurea*)
Scarlet runner bean (*Phaseolus coccineus*)

COMPACT GROWERS
Sweet pea (*Lathyrus odoratus*)
Black-eyed Susan vine (*Thunbergia alata*)
Vining nasturtium (*Tropaeolum majus*)

FLOWERING VINES WITH FRAGRANCE FOR HOUSE OR GARDEN

It isn't just in fairy tales that fragrant flowering vines creep near an open window for the amusement of a princess-heroine. Install a trellis at your home and clothe it with one of these fragrant flowering vines.

Kolomikta vine (*Actinidia Kolomikta*)
Five-leaf akebia (*Akebia quinata*)
Sweet autumn clematis (*Clematis maximowicziana*)
Moonflower (*Ipomoea alba*)
Sweet pea (*Lathyrus odoratus*)
Hall's honeysuckle (*Lonicera japonica* 'Halliana')
Winter honeysuckle (*Lonicera fragrantissima*)
Silver lace vine (*Polygonum Aubertii*)
Wisteria (*Wisteria* spp.)

NATIVE VINES

North America has generated some interesting vines right in our own fields and woodlands.

PERENNIAL NATIVE VINES

Trumpet vine (*Campsis radicans*)   Passion
Virgin's bower (*Clematis virginiana*)   Flower
Bay star vine (*Schisandra glabra*)
Frost grape (*Vitis vulpina*)
Kentucky wisteria (*Wisteria macrostachys*)
American wisteria (*Wisteria frutescens*)

ANNUAL NATIVE VINES

Passion flower (*Passiflora incarnata*)

A RAINBOW OF FLOWERING VINES

No matter what your landscape color scheme, there is a vine to suit it. Clematis are especially easy to blend into any color group, such is the diversity of that wonderful flowering vine.

YELLOW FLOWERS

Yellow trumpet vine (*Campsis radicans* 'Flava')
Yellow trumpet honeysuckle (*Lonicera sempervirens* 'Sulphurea')
Vining nasturtium (*Tropaeolum majus*)
Canary creeper (*Tropaeolum peregrinum*)

ORANGE TO RED FLOWERS

Trumpet creeper (*Campsis radicans*)
Red morning glory (*Ipomoea coccinea*)
Dropmore Scarlet Brown's honeysuckle (*Lonicera* × *Brownii* 'Dropmore Scarlet')
Coral honeysuckle (*Lonicera sempervirens*)
Nasturtium (*Tropaeolum majus*)

PINK TO RED FLOWERS

Nelly Moser clematis (*Clematis* 'Nelly Moser')
Scarlet runner bean (*Phaseolus coccineus*)
Sweet pea (*Lathyrus odoratus*)

BLUE FLOWERS

Perle d'Azur clematis (*Clematis* 'Perle d'Azur')
Morning glory (*Ipomoea* 'Heavenly Blue')

WHITE FLOWERS

Henry clematis (*Clematis Henryi*)
Anemone clematis (*Clematis montana*)
Sweet autumn clematis (*Clematis maximowicziana*)

Virgin's bower (*Clematis virginiana*)
Climbing hydrangea (*Hydrangea petiolaris*)
Sweet pea (*Lathyrus odoratus*)
Silverlace vine (*Polygonum Aubertii*)
White Chinese wisteria (*Wisteria sinensis alba*)

PURPLE FLOWERS
Jackman clematis (*Clematis Jackmanii*)
Wisteria (*Wisteria* spp.)

NEW CULTIVARS OF VINES

Wholesale Bailey Nurseries, Inc. of St. Paul, Minnesota, stays in the know about new vines, hardy to climatic Zone 5. You may be able to have your local garden center order them for you. Here are a few from their 1997 catalog.

Engleman ivy (*Parthenocissus quinquefolia* var. *Engelmannii*)
Like Virginia ivy but with smaller leaves, less vigor, and better masonry clinging power.
Mme Galen trumpetvine (*Campsis* × *Tagliabuana* 'Mme Galen')
Hybrid with apricot-colored flowers in summer and fall.
Elegans porcelain berry (*Ampelopsis brevipedunculata* 'Elegans')
Leaves are slightly smaller than the species and emerge pink expanding to lovely white variegation. Traditional porcelain berries are also included.

GROUND COVERS

The term *ground cover* embraces a large group of herbaceous and evergreen plants, usually of modest height, that spread over a fairly wide area to form a dense mat of foliage. Many Midwesterners are familiar with perennial ground cover vines such as periwinkle (*Vinca minor*), English ivy (*Hedera* spp.), and *Pachysandra*. But there also are annual flowers, such as 'Purple Wave' (*Petunia* spp.), that serve as ground covers and ground cover roses like 'Alba Meidiland' and 'Red Meidiland'. Additionally, upright, clumping perennials like daylilies and ornamental grasses can be planted close together to fill space like a ground cover.

No matter what their origins or habits, ground covers are a wonderful way to paint broad strokes of greenery across a large garden, beneath trees, around shrubs, or amid upright perennials. Like a thick plush carpet, they form an intermediate step between lawn and garden, covering open soil with greenery and helping to squeeze out weeds.

A common mistake is the assumption that ground covers are no-maintenance plants, growing well under any condition and requiring no care. This isn't always the case. You must begin with a ground cover ideally suited to your soil and site. Plant it thickly enough to allow rapid coverage then water, weed, and fertilize as needed to encourage rapid establishment and growth. Only after a strong start will vigorous ground cover plants truly become easy-care.

Right Plant, Right Place

One prerequisite for lush, ground covering growth is finding the right plant for the location. Typically, ground covers such as ivy, periwinkle, and pachysandra are relegated to dark areas under trees where lawn grasses grow sparsely or not at all. Don't limit yourself only to the standards but consider other options as well. For example, the quiet shade beneath a mature oak can glow with bright silver markings on Beacon Silver lamium (*Lamium maculatum* 'Beacon Silver').

A wonderful variety of plants you may not have previously considered can serve as ground covers in sun. With arms outflung and resting along the warm soil, ground-hugging roses open glossy blooms to the sun. On a gravel bank beside a road—difficult to reach with a hose—Dragon's Blood sedum (*Sedum spurium* 'Dragon's Blood') entertains passing motorists with crimson flowers most of the summer. An abundance of considerations for different sites follows.

AGGRESSIVE SPREADING GROUND COVERS

Release these beasts with due caution. Once running rampant through your soil, they may be difficult to eradicate. One option for the cautious is to put them in beds surrounded by walls or paving, limits that will put a sure stop to their spread.

Goutweed (*Aegopodium Podagraria*)
Five-leaf akebia (*Akebia quinata*)
Chameleon houttuynia (*Houttuynia cordata* 'Chameleon')
Japanese honeysuckle (*Lonicera japonica*)
Creeping jenny (*Lysimachia Nummularia*)

Creeping
Jenny

GROUND COVERS FOR SUN AND MIXED BEDS

Letting a few, choice spreading plants fill an entire sunny bed makes a simple and bold landscape element. In sunny areas, ground covers also can be used to edge the lawn or spread along the sidewalk. When blending with other plants, use ground covers that spread at a modest pace (marked with an asterisk). They are less likely to overwhelm slower growing plants.

*Prostrate abelia (*Abelia* × *grandiflora* 'Prostrata')
Bugleweed (*Ajuga* spp.)
*Plumbago (*Ceratostigma plumbaginoides*)
Cotoneaster (*Cotoneaster Dammeri* and *horizontalis*)
Wintercreeper (*Euonymus Fortunei*)
*Hardy geraniums (*Geranium* spp.)
*Daylilies (*Hemerocallis* hyb.)
Creeping St. John's wort (*Hypericum calycinum*)
Creeping junipers (*Juniperus* spp.)
*Maiden grass (*Miscanthus* spp.)
*Catmint (*Nepeta* spp.)
*Creeping phlox (*Phlox subulata*)
Knotweed (*Polygonum capitatum*)
Three-toothed cinquefoil (*Potentilla tridentata*)
Dragon's blood stonecrop (*Sedum spurium* 'Dragon's Blood')
Lamb's ear (*Stachys byzantina*)
*Creeping thymes (*Thymus* spp.)

GROUND COVERS FOR SHADE

Almost every yard has some shade lying beneath trees or on the north side of the house. Ground covers can make that space as lush as sunnier areas. An abundance of plants will grow in light shade, places with dappled sun, or some morning or late afternoon sun. But full shade is the perfect place for some ground covers shine.

LIGHT SHADE

Bugleweed (*Ajuga* spp.)
European ginger (*Asarum europaeum*)
Wild ginger (*Asarum* spp.)
Bergenia (*Bergenia* spp.)
Golden star (*Chrysogonum virginianum*)
Epimedium (*Epimedium* spp.)
English ivy (*Hedera helix*)
Hostas (*Hosta* spp.)
Yellow archangel (*Lamiastrum Galeobdolon*)
Dead nettle (*Lamium maculatum*)
Siberian cypress (*Microbiota decussata*)
Pachysandra (*Pachysandra* spp.)
Boston ivy (*Parthenocissus tricuspidata*)
Woodland phlox (*Phlox divaricata*)
Periwinkle (*Vinca minor*)

European Ginger

DEEP SHADE

In the very dark shade under a thickly branched pine tree, sometimes the best look comes from a neat carpet of mulch, which has no need for light. Under deciduous trees, you can try one of two options. Use shade-loving evergreen ground covers or try spreading woodland wild flowers (marked with an asterisk) that take advantage of the spring sun and hold their foliage into summer. The two aren't always compatible. Often more aggressive ivies and periwinkles will smother more ephemeral wildflowers—a common problem in Midwestern woodlands infested with escaped ivies from adjoining shade gardens.

*Wild ginger (*Asarum canadense*)
Lily-of-the-valley (*Convallaria majalis*)
Sweet woodruff (*Galium odoratum*)
English ivy (*Hedera helix*)
Pachysandra (*Pachysandra terminalis*)
Boston ivy (*Parthenocissus tricuspidata*)
*Foamflower (*Tiarella cordifolia*)
Periwinkle (*Vinca minor*)
*Violets (*Viola* spp.)
*Mayapple (*Podophyllum peltatum*)

Foamflower

"Around a series of hydrangea plants I have two marvelous ground covers—strawberry begonias (*Saxifraga stolonifera*) and hardy begonias (*Begonia grandis*). Both are moderate spreaders with handsome foliage and novel enough to be of interest."
    Edgar Gildenhaus, former editor of Garden Life, *monthly newsletter of the St. Louis Horticultural Society*

GROUND COVERS FOR DRY SOILS

Succulents and drought tolerant plants can make interesting and low maintenance ground covers in dry areas, places that are sandy or hard to irrigate.

Pussy-toes (*Antennaria dioica*)
Sea thrift (*Armeria maritima*)
Daylilies (*Hemerocallis* spp.)
Creeping St. John's wort (*Hypericum calycinum*)
Creeping junipers (*Juniperus horizontalis, J. conferta,* and *J. procumbens*)
Moss pink (*Phlox subulata*)
Sedums (*Sedum* spp.)
Lamb's ear (*Stachys byzantina*)
Creeping thymes (*Thymus* spp.)
Yucca (*Yucca filamentosa*)

NATIVE GROUND COVERS

Who wouldn't be proud to say that a thriving sweep of plants is an All-American ground cover? Using native plants also encourages you to dabble in more unusual species, striking and memorable in the garden.

Wood anemone (*Anemone quinquefolia*)
Pussy-toes (*Antennaria plantaginifolia*)
Shuttleworth's ginger (*Asarum Shuttleworthii*)
Bunchberry (*Cornus canadensis*)
Sharp-lobed hepatica (*Hepatica acutiloba*)
Twinflower (*Linnaea borealis*)
Wild lily-of-the-valley (*Maianthemum canadense*)
Partridge berry (*Mitchella repens*)
Foam flower (*Tiarella cordifolia* var. *cordifolia*)
Barren strawberry (*Waldsteinia fragarioides*)

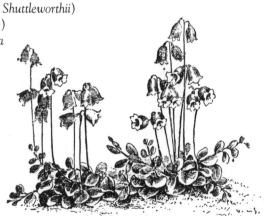

Twinflower

JOE OPPE'S CLASSICS

Joe Oppe, horticulturist at Des Moines Botanical Garden in Iowa, finds weather strongly influences his selection of ground covers. Winters are long and often very cold, a time that English ivy foliage can be burnt back to the ground. Spring and early summer can be very wet, encouraging root rot where soils are not well drained. Summers can be just the opposite—hot and dry. The following ground covers tolerate—even thrive—despite this abuse.

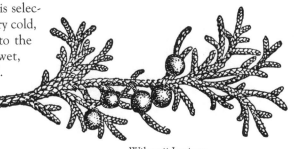

Wiltonii Juniper

Bugleweed (*Ajuga reptans*)
Lily-of-the-valley (*Convallaria* spp.)
Daylilies (*Hemerocallis* spp.)
Hosta (*Hosta* spp.)
Wiltonii juniper (*Juniperus horizontalis* 'Wiltonii')
Periwinkle (*Vinca minor*)

GROUND COVERS FOR A SLOPE

I twice tried mowing a short bank beside the drainage ditch at my old house. Holding the push mower firmly, I slowly let it roll down the hillside—and nearly lost my footing and fell as the full weight of the mower hit me with a jerk. Then I tried pushing the mower up the bank, but after two grunting and groaning passes, I was so exhausted that I quit. Ground covers that need no mowing make much easier options for slopes.

Jump start slope plantings by making sure there is good topsoil—not just eroded clay— and enough moisture or irrigation to help the plants get started. If transforming a grassy slope, till and plant small plots so the whole slope is not laid bare and susceptible to erosion. When a new ground cover planting is well established, expand it into nearby areas. Banks that are already suffering from erosion can be terraced and enriched with new topsoil before planting.

Cotoneasters, low (*Cotoneaster* spp.)
Wintercreeper (*Euonymus Fortunei*)
English ivy (*Hedera helix*)
Daylilies (*Hemerocallis* spp.)
Creeping junipers (*Juniperus* spp.)
Pachysandra (*Pachysandra terminalis*)
Virginia creeper (*Parthenocissus quinquefolia*)
Memorial rose (*Rosa Wichuraiana*)
Rugosa rose (*Rosa rugosa*)
Periwinkle (*Vinca minor*)

MIDWEST GROUND COVER'S TRIED-AND-TRUE RECOMMENDATIONS

Midwest Ground Covers, a St. Charles, Illinois, wholesale nursery specializing in ground covers, has been selling most of the following ground covers for twenty-six years. Their plants have survived intense cold, little snow, and hot sticky summers and have remained heavily in demand—a good recommendation indeed.

DECIDUOUS GROUND COVERS
Carpet bugle (*Ajuga genevensis*)
Bronze carpet bugle (*Ajuga reptans* 'Atropurpurea')
Braunherz carpet bugle (*Ajuga reptans* 'Braunherz')
Burgundy Glow carpet bugle (*Ajuga reptans* 'Burgundy Glow')
Jungle Beauty carpet bugle (*Ajuga reptans* 'Jungle Beauty Improved')
Silver Beauty carpet bugle (*Ajuga reptans* 'Silver Beauty')
Sweet woodruff (*Galium odoratum*)
Variegated yellow archangel (*Lamiastrum Galeobdolon* 'Florentium')
Bird's foot trefoil (*Lotus corniculatus*)
Dwarf fleece flower (*Polygonum Reynoutria*)
Creeping buttercup (*Ranunculus repens*)
Stonecrop (*Sedum acre* and *album*)
Bailey's Gold stonecrop (*Sedum* 'Bailey's Gold')
Kamtschaticum stonecrop (*Sedum kamtschaticum*)
Iceberg stonecrop (*Sedum rupestre* 'Forsleranum')
Dragon's blood stonecrop (*Sedum spurium* 'Dragon's Blood')
Tricolor stonecrop (*Sedum spurium* 'Tri-color')
Hens and chicks (*Sempervivum* spp.)
Barren strawberry (*Waldsteinia ternata*)

EVERGREEN GROUND COVERS
Purple leaf wintercreeper (*Euonymus Fortunei* var. *coloratus*)
Small leaf wintercreeper (*Euonymus Fortunei* 'Minimus')
Bulgarian ivy (*Hedera helix* 'Bulgaria')
Thorndale English ivy (*Hedera helix* 'Thorndale')
Small leaf Baltic ivy (*Hedera helix* 'Wilson')
Pachysandra (*Pachysandra terminalis* 'Green Carpet' and 'Green Sheen')
Periwinkle (*Vinca minor*)
White periwinkle (*Vinca minor* 'Alba')
Purple periwinkle (*Vinca minor* 'Atropurpurea')
Bowles periwinkle (*Vinca minor* 'Bowles Variety')
Darts Blue periwinkle (*Vinca minor* 'Darts Blue')
Ralph Shugert periwinkle (*Vinca minor* 'Ralph Shugert')

"This is a pretty harsh environment—a difficult climate and clay soil. What makes it even more difficult is that people tend to use ground covers where little else will grow. While many ground covers will take this treatment, European ginger (*Asarum europaeum*) and a few others won't."

Kathy Freeland, Midwest Ground Covers in St. Charles, Illinois

Ground Covers through the Seasons

Many ground covers exhibit seasonal change. The foliage may emerge tinted chartreuse or ruby in spring, followed by festive summer flowers, and perhaps brilliant foliage in fall.

If you look closely, even English ivy, grown in never-ending carpets of darkest green, changes with time. Young vines produce juvenile leaves that are five lobed and marked with white veins, distinctly different from more rounded adult leaves on older vines. Seemingly steadfast carpet junipers with green, gold, or silvery sheens in spring, summer, and fall may change in winter to bronze or burgundy.

GROUND COVERS FOR AUTUMN FOLIAGE COLOR

When overhead tree leaves begin to turn bronze, gold, red, and orange in autumn, some deciduous ground covers will do the same. Their interplay can make fascinating color echoes.

Plumbago (*Ceratostigma plumbaginoides*)
Cotoneaster, low (*Cotoneaster* spp.)
Creeping geranium (*Geranium macrorrhizum*)
Creeping mahonia (*Mahonia repens*)
Woodbine (*Parthenocissus inserta*)
Virginia creeper (*Parthenocissus quinquefolia*)

EVERGREEN GROUND COVERS

Those who miss the greenery of summer in the dregs of winter can save themselves the expense of a trip to Florida. Instead, plant verdant evergreen ground covers for your winter eyeful of chlorophyll.

European ginger (*Asarum europaeum*)
Winter creeper (*Euonymous Fortunei*)
English ivy (*Hedera helix*)
Creeping mahonia (*Mahonia repens*)
Pachysandra (*Pachysandra terminalis*)
Boston ivy (*Parthenocissus tricuspidata*)
Periwinkle (*Vinca minor*)

AN ANNUAL GROUND COVER FOR SUMMER AND FALL BLOOM
"'Purple Wave', an interspecific cross of two petunia species, is the first petunia of its type to grow 4 to 6 inches tall and 3 to 4 feet across. We recommend it for a ground cover because it grows so quickly and covers a lot of ground in one season. Because it's heat and drought tolerant, it will flower consistently all summer long with a minimal amount of care—exactly what you're looking for in a ground cover."
Nona Wolfram-Koivula, executive director of All America Selections, Downers Grove, Illinois

FLOWERING GROUND COVERS

Some of the most charming ground covers are those that add their blossoms to the mix of nearby flowering shrubs and trees. They are well worth adding to seasonal bloom lists as they cover the lowest strata of the garden while taller bloomers rise overhead. One of the nicest combinations I've seen is the starry white flowers of sweet woodruff billowing at the base of a white-flowered azalea in Kathleen Gips's garden in Chagrin Falls, Ohio. Other possibilities are limited only by the depth of a gardener's imagination. This list will get you started; add other ground covering perennials and shrubs as you discover them.

SPRING-FLOWERING GROUND COVERS

Bugleweed (*Ajuga* spp.)
Bergenia (*Bergenia* spp.)
Snow-in-summer (*Cerastium* spp.)
Lily-of-the-valley (*Convallaria majalis*)
Cranberry cotoneaster (*Cotoneaster apiculata*)
Royal Beauty cotoneaster (*Cotoneaster Dammeri* 'Royal Beauty')
Golden star (*Chrysogonum virginianum*)
Maiden pinks (*Dianthus deltoides*)
Epimedium (*Epimedium spp.*)
Sweet woodruff (*Galium odoratum*)
Yellow archangel (*Lamiastrum Galeobdolon*)
Lamium (*Lamium maculatum*)
Geranium, hardy (*Geranium* spp.)
Moss phlox (*Phlox subulata*)
Creeping phlox (*Phlox stolonifera*)
Lamb's ears (*Stachys byzantina*)
Periwinkle (*Vinca minor*)

SUMMER-FLOWERING GROUND COVERS

Chinese astilbe (*Astilbe chinensis* var. *pumila*)
Snow-in-summer (*Cerastium* spp.)
Plumbago (*Ceratostigma plumbaginoides*)
Maiden pinks (*Dianthus deltoides*)
Geranium, hardy (*Geranium* spp.)
Creeping baby's-breath (*Gypsophila repens*)
Daylilies (*Hemerocallis* spp.)
Hosta (*Hosta* spp.)
St. John's wort (*Hypericum calycinum*)
Purple Wave petunia (*Petunia* spp. 'Purple Wave')
Snakeweed (*Polygonum Bistorta*)
Cinquefoil (*Potentilla* spp.)
Roses, ground cover types (*Rosa* spp.)
Dragon's blood stonecrop (*Sedum spurium* 'Dragon's Blood')

FALL-FLOWERING GROUND COVERS

Japanese anemone (*Anemone* × *hybrida*)
Chinese astilbe (*Astilbe chinensis* var. *pumila*)
Plumbago (*Ceratostigma plumbaginoides*)

Purple Wave petunia (*Petunia* spp. 'Purple Wave')
Snakeweed (*Polygonum Bistorta*)
Roses, ground cover types (*Rosa* spp.)

Ground Covers in the Landscape

My new house lies on 2½ acres, all open lawn crying out for gardens. Until the time comes when I can afford the extensive list of plants I've decided I simply must have, I will fill the beds with interesting ground covers. Easily divided and multiplied, they are a cost-effective way to make a barren yard interesting.

Ground covers also can't be beat for underplanting trees and shrubs. Common practice when planting trees and shrubs is to dig a hole in the lawn and plop the plant in. This seems easy at first but complications arise later. Young trees and shrubs are stunted by strenuous root competition with the grasses. Those that survive require regular handweeding to remove tall grasses in places the mower can't reach, and mowing too close to tender young trunks causes bark damage. In these and many other places around the yard, ground covers are waiting to come to the rescue.

GILBERT AND EMILY DANIELS'S LESS-COMMON GROUND COVERS

Whenever you visit an outstanding public or private garden, watch for interesting examples of plants used as ground covers. You can get wonderful ideas for your own yard. One such garden is in Indianapolis, where Emily and Gilbert Daniels (the latter a retired botanist) have a wonderful four-acre garden. Large freeform beds sweep beside lawn in sunny areas and extensive woodland plots cluster in the ravines surrounding the property. Ground covers, such as the following, grace both areas.

Lady's mantle (*Alchemilla mollis*)
Chinese astilbe (*Astilbe chinensis* var. *pumila*)
Pink Panda strawberries (*Fragaria* × 'Pink Panda')
Serenata red flowered strawberry (*Fragaria* × 'Serenata')
Sweet woodruff (*Galium odoratum*)
Daylilies (*Hemerocallis* spp.)
Hosta, smaller species and cultivars
    (*Hosta* spp. 'August Moon', 'Royal Standard', 'Kabitan', 'Golden Tiara')
St. John's wort (*Hypericum calycinum*)
Allegheny pachysandra (*Pachysandra procumbens*)

"A ground cover, a large swath of a single species, allows you to spread a consistent texture and color over large areas, and we like that look. We learn which plants will work best by experimenting. We are seldom pleased the first time we plant something new. We usually end up moving it around and trying again a time or two before we are satisfied."

Emily and Gilbert Daniels, Indianapolis, Indiana

GROUND COVERS THAT DRAPE AND TRAIL

Plants that spread across the earth may also form a beautiful spray that cascades over walls and banks in a soft waterfall of color. This always brings to mind the lovely weeping forsythias at Stan Hywet Hall in Akron, Ohio. They cover six-foot-high brick retaining walls, clothing them with golden flowers in spring and greenery in summer.

> Rock cress (*Arabis caucasica* and *Aubrieta deltoidea*)
> Hardy alyssum (*Aurinia saxatilis*)
> Cotoneasters, low (*Cotoneaster* spp.)
> Wintercreeper (*Euonymous Fortunei*)
> Weeping forsythia (*Forsythia suspensa*)
> Candytuft (*Iberis sempervirens*)
> English ivy (*Hedera helix*)
> Creeping junipers (*Juniperus* spp.)
> Creeping thyme (*Thymus* spp.)
> Periwinkle (*Vinca minor*)

GROUND COVERS FOR FRONT OF THE BORDER

Painting a neat low sweep of foliage along the front of any garden gives it a sense of order. If the front-runners are ground covers that spread modestly (such as those listed below), you can divide and multiply them repeatedly to cover the foreground of even the largest bed. Choose ground covers that look good year round, since they will be displayed in such prominence. Avoid ground covers that spread so aggressively that they choke out neighboring plants.

> Wooly yarrow (*Achillea tomentosa*)
> Bugleweed (*Ajuga* spp.)
> Lady's mantle (*Alchemilla mollis*)
> Sea pink (*Armeria maritima*)
> Bergenia (*Bergenia cordifolia*)
> Plumbago (*Ceratostigma plumbaginoides*)
> Epimedium (*Epimedium* spp.)
> Hardy geraniums (*Geranium* spp.)
> Lamium (*Lamium maculatum*)
> Creeping lilyturf (*Liriope spicata*)
> Moss phlox (*Phlox subulata*)
> Foam flower (*Tiarella cordifolia*)

GROUND COVERS WITH COLORFUL FOLIAGE

Handsome foliage becomes more important than ever when planting large masses of ground covers.Ground covers with variations on green—blue or golden blushes, silver variegation, or red and pink highlights—add sparkle to dark areas.

BLUE FOLIAGE
> Creeping junipers, blue leaf (*Juniperus* spp.)
> Hosta, blue leaf (*Hosta* spp.)
> Creeping mahonia (*Mahonia repens*)

WHITE OR CREAM VARIEGATION

Silver Beauty bugleweed (*Ajuga reptans* 'Silver Beauty')
Harlequin euonymus (*Euonymus Fortunei* 'Harlequin')
Ivory Jade euonymus (*Euonymus Fortunei* 'Ivory Jade')
Hosta, variegated (*Hosta* spp.)
Variegated dead nettle (*Lamiastrum Galeobdolon* 'Variegatum'
or 'Herman's Pride')
Beacon Silver henbit (*Lamium maculatum* 'Beacon Silver')
Variegated pachysandra (*Pachysandra terminalis* 'Variegata')
Lamb's ears (*Stachys byzantina*)
Ralph Shugert periwinkle (*Vinca minor* 'Ralph Shugert')

YELLOW FOLIAGE

Sparkle 'n Gold euonymus (*Euonymus Fortunei* 'Spargozam')
Hosta, yellow leaf (*Hosta* spp.)
Creeping junipers, yellow leaf (*Juniperus* spp.)
Beedham's White lamium (*Lamium maculatum* 'Beedham's White')
Variegated yucca (*Yucca filamentosa* 'Bright Edge')

PINK, PURPLE, OR RED FOLIAGE

Bronze Beauty bugleweed (*Ajuga reptans* 'Bronze Beauty')
Burgundy Glow ajuga (*Ajuga reptans* 'Burgundy Glow')
Purple leaf wintercreeper (*Euonymus Fortunei* var. *coloratus*)
Tricolor sedum (*Sedum spurium* 'Tri-color')
Dragon's blood stonecrop (*Sedum spurium* 'Dragon's Blood')
Ruby Mantle sedum (*Sedum spurium* 'Ruby Mantle')
Purple hen and chicks (*Sempervivum* spp. 'Purpureum')
Purple Labrador violet (*Viola labradorica* var. *purpurea*)

ROSES

Roses have a way of sneaking up on people. Some unassuming gardeners begin innocently enough, growing one or two roses, not realizing how easy it is to catch the bug. Enticed by rose catalogs and garden center displays, they buy a few more roses—just to get some different colors. Before you know it, there are a couple dozen roses filling up the former vegetable garden or sweeping a swath through the perennial garden. Rose addiction is easier than ever to catch thanks to the rapidly expanding selection of pest and disease-resistant cultivars.

Landscape roses are hardy, disease resistant, and don't require regular spraying or frequent replacement—big pluses in my book. Some of the best roses for the Midwest are

A ROSE RUNDOWN
     With so many different kinds of roses, how can one tell them all apart? Let this list be your guide, realizing that there are overlaps among these general classes.

HISTORIC ROSES
Gallica roses; full-flowered late-spring bloomers with pink and purple flowers and a wonderful fragrance
Damask roses; intensely fragrant late-spring bloomers; autumn damasks may rebloom if cut back properly
Moss roses; famous for their full round flowers, sticky with fragrant oils

MODERN ROSES
Hybrid teas; graceful tear drop-shaped flowers but some have lost their fragrance
Grandiflorus; similar but with longer stems good for cutting
Polyanthas and *Floribundas*; clusters of smaller flowers that can make nice landscape roses
Landscape roses; combine the durability and fragrance of older roses with repeat blooming habit of newer types

coming from David Austin of England, House of Meilland in France, Town and Country of Denmark, and Agriculture Canada. Like all roses, landscape roses need high-performance growing conditions—rich, well-drained soil and full sun.

Polyantha roses have clusters of smaller flowers on low-growing bushes; they are easily blended into sunny shrub borders or flower gardens. *Miniature roses*, which are roses shrunken to a fraction of their previous size, are ideal for pots or baskets or for blending with annual flowers. Old-fashioned or *antique roses*, including the famous apothecary, moss, Damask, and York and Lancaster roses of history, bring a bit of the past into gardens of today. *Climbing roses*, which may need winter protection, add romance to a garden as they climb arbors or ramble along fences.

Right Plant, Right Place

Roses, with very few exceptions, languish in anything less than full sun and rich, well-drained soil so I can't recommend trying to push the limits and grow them in shade. If you have Midwestern clay, enrich it by adding bountiful organic matter until the soil becomes loose and spongy. Some roses require a lot of care to keep them going. If you don't have time to primp primadonna roses, select a disease resistant and thoroughly hardy rose from those that follow.

Carolina Rose

LOW- OR NO-SPRAY ROSES

In Treasure Island, a pirate given the black spot knew death was imminent. In the rose garden, the arrival of black spot disease means much trouble for rose and gardener alike. Spotted leaves must be painstakingly picked up and destroyed to discourage reinfection, and the rose must be sprayed regularly with a preventative fungicide or several different fungicides applied in rotation.

It just makes so much more sense, at least to this lazy gardener, to start with roses that naturally resist diseases like black spot. There are dozens of disease-resistant roses available presently and more coming out every year. Here is just a sampling.

DISEASE-RESISTANT LANDSCAPE SHRUB ROSES
'Aspen'
'Cape Cod'
'Carefree Beauty'
'Central Park'
'Cherry Meidiland'
'Eden'
'Newport'
'Pink Meidiland'
'Scarlet Meidiland'
'Sea Foam'
'White Meidiland'

DISEASE-RESISTANT CLIMBING ROSES
'John Davis'
'Polka'
'New Dawn'
'William Baffin'

DISEASE-RESISTANT HYBRID TEA ROSES
'Brandy'
'Christopher Columbus'
'Harry G. Hastings'
'Kentucky Derby'
'Paradise'
'Pascali'

OTHER DISEASE-RESISTANT ROSES
'Betty Prior' (Floribunda)
'Europeana' (Floribunda)
'The Fairy' (Polyantha)
'Kathleen' (Musk rose)
Rosa alba (Antique rose)
Rosa rugosa 'Albo-plena' (Rugosa rose)
Rosa rugosa 'Belle Poitevine' (Rugosa rose)
Memorial rose (*Rosa Wichuraiana*) (Ground cover)

BOB CARDE'S FAVORITE AUSTIN ROSES

David Austin's New English Roses—fragrant, vigorous, bright, and long blooming—are the darlings of the rose world. But can they hold up to a frigid Midwestern winter? An affirmative answer comes from Bob Carde, amateur rose grower from Homewood, Illinois, who has been experimenting with Austin hybrid roses for the past five years. Despite cold Chicago-area winters with little snow cover and high winds, the following cultivars have proven reliably hardy and entirely worth growing.

'Heritage'	Large, blush pink flowers
'Graham Thomas'	Yellow flowers
'Abraham Darby'	Apricot flowers, most floriferous
'Squire'	Low-growing, red flowers
'Mary Rose'	Very floriferous, pink flowers
'L.D. Braithwaite'	Cerise flowers

"In my yard, where the cold north wind comes whipping down the road in winter, some of the branches of Austin roses can break off and make the plants a little scraggly in spring. To reduce this problem, I usually cut them back to three-feet high in fall. Some rebound in summer to grow eight-feet high, but judicious pruning keeps them in check. The particularly difficult winter of '95–'96 caused them to die back to the ground; fortunately, they recovered and gave a good display the following summer."

Bob Carde, rose enthusiast in Homewood, Illinois

EXTRA HARDY ROSES

For northern climates where roses sometimes mascarade as annuals, try an extra hardy rose from the following list. Look for the many good choices from Agriculture Canada as well.

Nearly Wild rose (*Rosa* 'Nearly Wild')
Redleaf rose (*Rosa rubrifolia*)
Rugosa rose (*Rosa rugosa*)
Virginia rose (*Rose virginiana*)

SUSAN SIFRITT'S FAVORITE OLD-FASHIONED ROSES

With a Doctorate in Geography and a Masters of Library Science, guess what Susan Sifritt likes to do with her spare time? She grows roses, for herself and for the Shaker Heights (Ohio) Community Rose Garden, which has about 1600 roses of 175 types. When the garden was started, Sifritt dug into local rose history to help come up with appropriate roses and a design similar to a 1925 rose garden that once occupied the same site. She laments that some early roses have been lost and that others aren't hardy. But the following cultivars have made it through Shaker Heights winter with flying colors.

'Gruss An Aachen'	White floribunda
'La Reine Victoria'	Very fragrant bourbon
'Mme. Hardy'	Fragrant, white damask
'Moss Salet'	Repeat bloomer
'Mrs. John Lang'	Fragrant and disease-resistant hybrid perpetual
Rosa mundi 'Gallica'	Red stripe over pink
'Topaz Jewel'	Yellow rugosa

 "We always try to buy roses that are growing on their own roots instead of on grafts, which are less hardy. I've also found it's better to order roses for fall planting because the weather is more predictable then. Be careful if you buy them in spring from California, because the roses arrive in February or March before you can use them."
Susan Sifritt, Ph.D., Shaker Heights Community Rose Garden, Shaker Heights, Ohio

NORMAN BACKUS' FAVORITE HARDY MINIATURE ROSES

Don't let their petite appearances fool you, most miniature roses are good and hardy. Norman Backus, a life consulting rosarian and life judge with the American Rose Society, has been growing some the following miniature roses (as well as other types) in Valparaiso, Indiana, for the past decade.

'Fair Hope'	'Green Ice'
'Kathy Robinson'	'Kitty Hawk'
'Irrestible'	'Lavender Jewel'
'Magic Carousel'	'Minnie Pearl'

'Red Beauty'   'Regine'
'Rise and Shine'   'Snow Bride'

HARDY CLIMBING ROSES

There may be nothing that sets the heart of a flower lover beating more quickly than a climbing rose dripping flowers from a trellis or rambling along a fence. Unfortunately, in much of the Midwest, many climbing roses are not reliably hardy. Minnesota rose growers are known to dig trenches and bury their climbing roses for winter protection. If this seems like too much work for you, consider growing some of the new, extra hardy Explorer climbers bred in Canada. (Also see Paul Jerebek's roses in this chapter.)

'Captain Samuel Holland'   'David Thompson'
'Jens Munk'   'John Cabot'
'Martin Frobisher'   'William Baffin'

Roses through the Seasons

Just as some of us have gotten used to microwaving popcorn in three minutes and e-mailing messages in ten seconds, we've come to expect roses to bloom, and bloom, and bloom, saturating the garden with nonstop color. But many old-fashioned roses and wild species roses only bloom once—usually in early summer.

ROSE HIPS FOR SUMMER AND FALL

A distant relative of apples, roses may produce red or orange fruits after their flowers fade. These fruits are called *rose hips*. High in vitamin C, they are often used in herbal teas for their tart, citruslike flavor. Until harvested, they look great on rose bushes. Some particularly interesting hips grow on the following.

Konigin von Danemarck rose (*Rosa alba* 'Konigin von Danemarck')
Dog rose (*R. canina*)
Carolina rose (*Rosa carolina*)
Empress Josephine Gallica rose (*Rosa Gallica* 'Empress Josephine')
Redleaf rose (*Rosa glauca*)
Kathleen hybrid musk (*Rosa* 'Kathleen')
Nymphenburg rose (*Rosa* 'Nymphenburg')
Pink Meidiland rose (*Rosa* 'Pink Meidiland')
Rugosa rose (*Rosa rugosa*)
Frau Dagmar Hastrup rugosa (*Rosa rugosa* 'Frau Dagmar Hastrup')

Dog Rose

OLD-FASHIONED ROSES FOR JUNE BLOOM

Absence makes the heart grow fonder, and this may explain why some gardeners are avid fans of old-fashioned roses that bloom only once—in early June. More importantly, however, some of these fragrant flowers have been beloved for centuries.

> Cabbage rose (*Rosa centifolia*)
> Damask roses (*Rosa damascena*)
> Gallica roses (*Rosa Gallica*)
> Moss roses (*Rosa centifolia*)

ROSES FOR HANDSOME FALL COLOR

Although roses are not known for their fall color, a few do turn attractive shades of yellow or orange and can add to the seasonal display.

> Frau Dagmar Hastrup (*Rosa rugosa* 'Frau Dagmar Hastrup')
> Prairie rose (*Rosa setigera*)
> Virginia rose (*Rosa virginiana*)

ATTRACTIVE WINTER INTEREST

It's a real treat to find a rose that looks good in winter. Such is the case with the following roses.

'Therese Burgnet' (*Rosa rugosa* 'Therese Burgnet')	Red canes
Redleaf rose (*Rosa glauca*)	Purple canes
Virginia rose (*Rosa virginiana*)	Red canes

Roses in the Landscape

Until recently, roses usually held reign in their own, usually formal, gardens. But today, with all the different kinds of roses available, they can go just about anywhere in the yard (as long as growing conditions are right).

ROSES OF CLEAR COLORS

Roses come in a rainbow of colors, everything but clear blue. When blending them with other plants in the landscape, color planning can be simplified by using roses of clear colors. Pure shades of white (not ivory), red (not orange-red), pink (not mauve, lavender, or salmon-pink), and yellow (not orange-gold) are less likely to suffer from color conflicts.

TRUE RED ROSES

'Kentucky Derby'	(Hybrid tea)
'Mister Lincoln'	(Hybrid tea)
'Napa Valley'	(Town and Country rose)
'Olympiad'	(Hybrid tea)
'Othello'	(Austin rose)
'Scarlet Meidiland'	(Landscape rose)

TRUE PINK ROSES

'Bonica'	(Landscape rose)
'Cape Cod'	(Town and Country rose)
'Heritage'	(Austin)
'Katheryn Morley'	(Austin)
'Natchez'	(Town and Country rose)
'Queen Nephertii'	(Austin)

TRUE YELLOW ROSES

'Aspen'	(Town and Country rose)
Father Hugo rose	(*Rosa Hugonis*)
'Graham Thomas'	(Austin rose)
'The Pilgrim'	(Austin rose)

TRUE WHITE ROSES

'Fair Bianca'	(Austin rose)
Albo-plena	(*Rosa rugosa* 'Albo-plena')
Blanc Double de Coubert	(*Rosa rugosa* 'Blanc Double de Coubert')

RARE PAUL JERABEK'S ROSES

If you like to be the first person on the block to have a new rose, then the following will be perfect for your landscape. These are new introductions from Paul Jerabek, a rose breeder from northeastern Ohio who develops roses with bold colors and robust constitutions specifically for Midwestern conditions. These are available exclusively from Freedom Gardens, PO Box 161, Rootstown, Ohio 44272.

'Aunt Ruth'	(Climber)
'Brown Study'	(Floribunda)
'The Clerk'	(Landscape rose)
'Kirtland'	(Landscape rose)
'Our Pearl'	(Climber)
'Paulspride'	(Climber)
'Peggy M'	(Landscape rose)
'Photogenic'	(Climber)
'Snowbelt'	(Polyantha)
'Winifred'	(Grandiflora)

"Some roses are rare because, like 'Narzisse'—a classically formed, maize-yellow hybrid tea originally introduced in 1942—they have disappeared from commerce. Others are old garden roses, such as the blush-cream hybrid perpetual 'Elisa Boelle', that are available in Europe but still unknown in the United States. Still others, including the new introductions of Kirtland, Ohio, hybridizer Paul Jerabek, are rare simply because they are brand new."
Susan Schneider, Freedom Gardens, Portage County, Ohio

ROSES FOR CUTTING

My grandfather, an avid gardener, grew the most glorious hybrid tea roses in a hedge-enclosed garden behind his house in Dayton, Ohio. He always had a few stems of exquisitely tear-drop shaped rose buds on his kitchen counter and dining room table.

Roses are elegant cut flowers, useful as a single bloom in a bud vase, several stems blended with other flowers, or an armful filling a large urn. Some classic cut roses follow; add your own favorites as you experiment.

'Double Delight'
'Mister Lincoln'
'Monet'
'Olympiad'
'Pristine'
'Signature'
'Sonia'
'Touch of Class'
'Tropicana'

ROSES FOR EDGING

The edging of an ornamental garden, following the shape of the bed, may be its most prominent element. Why not use one of the following long-blooming, low-growing (1 to 2 feet) roses to give the edging pizzazz?

'Aspen'
'Central Park'
'English Garden'
'The Fairy'
'The Herbalist'
Miniature roses
'Natchez'

ROSES OF ANOTHER COLOR

Roses aren't called the queen of flowers for nothing. Some of the most dynamic looking roses feature several colors, two-tone blends, or bright stripes.

STRIPED ROSES

'Honorine de Brabant'	(Bourbon rose)
'Pinstripe'	(Miniature)
Rosa mundi	(Old-fashioned rose)
'Stars n' Stripes'	(Miniature)
'Tiger Tail'	(Floribunda)
'Variegata di Bologna'	(Bourbon rose)
'York and Lancaster'	(Old-fashioned rose)

TWO-TONED ROSES

'Climbing Peace'	(Climber)
'Chicago Peace'	(Hybrid tea)
'Double Delight'	(Hybrid tea)
'French Perfume'	(Hybrid tea)
'Monet'	(Hybrid tea)
'Peace'	(Hybrid tea)

FRAGRANT ROSES

The sweet perfume of a rose may have been the first element to catch the attention of mankind and initiate the beginning of a beautiful relationship. With fragrant essences distilled for perfumes, roses are classic fragrant plants. Some are more fragrant than others. Here is a sampling of roses that will appeal to your eyes and your nose.

Sweetbrier Rose

'Abraham Darby' (*Rosa* 'Abraham Darby')
'Bibi Maizoon' (*Rosa* 'Bibi Maizoon')
Bourbon roses (*Rosa* × *borboniana*)
'Constance Spry' (*Rosa* 'Constance Spry')
Sweetbrier (*Rosa Eglanteria*)
'Fair Bianca' (*Rosa* 'Fair Bianca')
French rose (*Rosa Gallica*)
'Graham Thomas' (*Rosa* 'Graham Thomas')
'Heritage' (*Rosa* 'Heritage')
'Mary Rose' (*Rosa* 'Mary Rose')
Musk rose (*Rosa moschata*)
'Zephirine Drouhin' (*Rosa moschata* 'Zephirine Drouhin')
'Blanc Double de Coubert' (*Rosa rugosa* 'Blanc Double de Coubert')
Memorial rose (*Rosa Wichuraiana*)

"There is no fragrance more heavenly than the old-fashioned roses. My favorite is 'Madame Isaac Pereire'. Among the old roses it is classified as an 1880 Bourbon. All summer the bush explodes into large mauve blossoms that perfume the yard and are noticed by everyone who passes by. Growing to eight feet in height, it fills the arbor with lush green, disease-free leaves and four-inch-wide, many-petaled flowers.

"The fragrance is heady and potent. When the petals are separated and dried, the faint scent of roses remains. The dried color is lavender-mauve, lovely in potpourri combined with lavender flowers and oak moss. The fragrance of this rose is completely preserved in rose petal jam, where the petals are cooked in a rose-flavored infusion. The jam is delicious in tea sandwiches or as a filling for cookies, although it seems unusual to taste the fragrance of roses!"

Kathleen Gips, author of Flora's Dictionary; The Victorian Language of Herbs and Flowers, *and owner of Pine Creek Herbs*

ROSES FOR BANKS

Two species of roses are particularly tough customers, able to cover ground and root aggressively enough to hold soil on a slope. Use them for a wonderful look on a bank.

Rugosa rose (*Rosa rugosa*)
Memorial rose (*Rosa Wichuraiana*)

ROSES FOR HEDGES

Landscape roses, if given the right site and soil, can be substituted for deciduous shrubs in an informal flowering hedge. What nicer way can there be to say "Stay out!" than with a beautiful flower—and a prickly branch. Plant these full-sized shrub roses close enough to intermingle and mature into a solid hedge.

MEDIUM-TALL SHRUB ROSES
Alba roses (*Rosa alba*)
Bonica (*Rosa* 'Bonica')
Moss roses (*Rosa centifolia*)
Pink Meidiland (*Rosa* 'Pink Meidiland')
Rugosa rose (*Rosa rugosa*)
'Winchester Cathedral' (*Rosa* 'Winchester Cathedral')

LARGE SHRUB ROSES
'Abraham Darby'
'Gertrude Jeckyll'
'Graham Thomas'
'L.D. Braithwaite'
'Othello'

HERBS AND EDIBLE ORNAMENTALS

A landscape can be beautiful and full of good things to eat by blending vegetables and herbs with flowers or giving decorative edibles their own space. It's easy to slip good-looking herbs such as pillow-shaped bush basil and silver-leaved garden sage into existing flower beds. As you pick bouquets, you can pinch off seasonings for the kitchen too. Flowering cabbage and kale with leaves colored quiet blue, bright white, and vivid purple-red can take the place of autumn annuals and chrysanthemums. Summer trellises dripping with red-flowered scarlet runner beans can create a privacy screen and yield yummy beans for dinner.

One of the Midwestern leaders in the use of ornamental edibles is the Chicago Botanic Garden; they practice what they preach with an entire island decked out in fruits and vegetables. Brilliant red, orange, and yellow 'Sweet Pickle' peppers blaze next to red salvias; asparagus forms a hedge dividing lecture areas from gardens; and fruit trees are shaped into geometric espaliers of all kinds. It's a great place to visit for ideas.

Whether you need to have a space-efficient garden or just enjoy having beautiful and edible crops around, you'll find the following lists especially useful. (Note: Because edible crops are easily found by their common names, the botanical name has been eliminated in these lists unless necessary to prevent confusion.)

Sweet
Cicely

Right Plant, Right Place

High-performance edible plants need the proper blend of sun and soil to produce the best possible results. Most high-performance herbs and vegetables require full sun, but with careful selection, you can also find interesting options for shade. Some examples follow.

ORNAMENTAL EDIBLES FOR SUN

If you've ever tried to grow vegetables in shade, you know how limiting it can be. Go for the gold—sunshine—with the following ornamental edibles.

Basil	attractive green to bronze leaves
Blueberries	white flowers, blue berries, red fall foliage
Cabbages	colorful foliage and heads
Chard, Swiss	colorful petioles
Chives	purple flowers
Chives, garlic	white flowers
Dill	frilly leaves, yellow flowers
Endive	frilly leaves
Eggplant	colorful fruit
Fennel	feathery leaves
Lavender	silver foliage, lavender flowers
Leaf lettuce	green to red leaves of assorted textures
Leeks	blue-green leaves
Parsley	frilly leaves
Peppers	colorful fruit
Sage	silver or other colored leaves
Tomato	colorful fruit

ORNAMENTAL EDIBLES FOR LIGHT SHADE

Some leafy vegetables and herbs (marked with an asterisk) are sun-lovers that will tolerate light shade and perform reasonably well there. Mints and sweet woodruff actually prefer it.

*Basil	attractive green to bronze leaves
*Blueberries	white flowers, blue berries, red fall foliage
*Chives	purple flowers
*Leaf lettuce	green to red leaves of assorted textures
Mint, pineapple	white variegated leaves
*Parsley	frilly leaves
Sweet cicely	ferny leaves
Sweet woodruff	fine foliage, creeping stems, white spring flowers

Leaf
Lettuce

ORNAMENTAL EDIBLES FOR DRY SITES

Herbs that originated in rocky or sandy soils of the Mediterranean and similar warm, dry regions grow best in lean soils. Since much of the Midwest is damp clay, these herbs perform best if grown in raised beds, behind dry stone retaining walls, beside well-drained walks, or in pots. Although young plants will need watering to keep the soil moist, once well established they seem to laugh off droughts.

Lavender	silver foliage, lavender flowers
Oregano	gold or green leaves, some with long-lasting flowers

Sage	silver, purple, or variegated leaves
Savory	narrow leaves, small flowers
Thyme	leaves marked silver, gold, and other colors, spring and early summer flowers

ORNAMENTAL EDIBLES FOR MOIST SITES

With the exception of water plants like arrowhead and water chestnuts, few ornamental edibles will grow in a marsh. But some lavish and succulent ornamental edibles, such as the following, prefer constantly moist soil.

Angelica	huge leaves and white flowers
Bee balm	spreading plant, colorful flowers
Mints	strong spreaders, small flowers
Rhubarb	broad leaves and red petioles
Sweet woodruff	fine foliage, creeping stems, white spring flowers

I've found it to be easier to grow pest-plagued crops amid the front yard flower beds, far away from the backyard vegetable garden. Flea beetles have trouble finding eggplants, and aphids are uncommon on Brussels sprouts camouflaged amid coneflowers.

Ornamental Edibles through the Seasons

More than perhaps any other class of plant, vegetables are inclined to come and go through the growing season, partly because you are harvesting them for the kitchen. Planning a sequence of plantings for spring, summer, and fall crops will keep the garden interesting and the refrigerator filled.

ORNAMENTAL EDIBLES FOR COOL SEASONS

Waiting to work the garden in spring can mean delaying until late May or early June by the time the spring rains stop and the clay dries out. To make the garden more accessible in April and ensure a good early vegetable crop, prepare your soil in fall or garden in a raised bed. If you miss the cool spring growing season, don't dispair. You can slip some of the same plants in during mid to late summer for fall harvest.

Cabbages	colorful foliage and heads
Chard, Swiss	colorful petioles
Chives	purple flowers
Endive	frilly leaves
Kale	colorful and frilly leaves
Leaf lettuce	green to red leaves of assorted textures
Parsley	frilly leaves

ORNAMENTAL EDIBLES FOR WARM, FROST-FREE WEATHER

In Cleveland and Chicago, mid May to Memorial Day are traditional planting times for summer-grown ornamental edibles that need frost-free weather to thrive. In the case of basil, even cool spring or fall temperatures in the 40s can damage flavor. The frost-free season ends in late September or October, depending on the latitude and year.

Basil	attractive green to bronze leaves
Beefsteak plant (*Perilla frutescens*)	green or purple leaves
Dill	frilly leaves, yellow flowers
Eggplant	colorful fruit
Geraniums, scented	divided to full leaves, sometimes variegated, with pink to lavender flowers
Peppers	colorful fruit
Tomato	colorful fruit

ORNAMENTAL EDIBLE PERENNIALS

Some of the most exciting ornamental edibles mascarade as perennial flowers. If spared from toxic sprays, their blossoms can be harvested for kitchen use. The following plants will live many years in the garden and flower for at least several weeks during the growing season.

Thyme

PERENNIALS WITH ATTRACTIVE, TASTY FLOWERS

Anise hyssop	lavender, blue, or purple flowers
Bee balm	white, red, purple, pink shaggy flowers
Chives	lavender flowers
Chives, garlic	white flowers
Daylilies	yellow, orange, red, pink, lavender, purple, cream flowers
Lavender	lavender flower spikes
Lovage	yellow flowers
Roses	pink, white, yellow, red, lavender flowers
Thyme	pink to lavender flowers

PERENNIALS WITH ATTRACTIVE FOLIAGE

There is more to ornamental and edible perennials than pretty flowers. Their attractive foliage can be blended into formal beds—as in a traditional herb garden—or more casual clusters of contrasting colors amid other shrubs and flowers. Leafy sprigs of all of the following except lavender can be harvested for teas or seasonings. Lavender sprigs are nice to dry for fragrant sachets and potpourri.

Lavender	silver foliage
Mint, pineapple	white variegated leaves
Thyme, variegated leaf types	yellow and white variegated leaves
Sage, purple leaved	purple leaves
Fennel, bronze	bronze leaves

ORNAMENTAL ANNUALS WITH COLORFUL FOLIAGE

Although annuals won't last as long as perennials, some have pretty and colorful foliage that looks great during the growing season. 'Blackie' sweet potato becomes a lush, tropical-looking vine in a class all its own.

Basil, purple	purple leaves
Cabbage, red	purple leaves
Lettuces, red	red leaves
Chard, Swiss	colorful petioles
Nasturtium, 'Alaska'	round, white variegated leaves
Perilla, purple leaf	purple leaves
Sage, tricolor	pink, white, and green leaves
Sweet potato, 'Blackie'	dark purple leaves

"With its very fine texture and deep green color, parsley provides a wonderful contrast to other vegetables or flowers of different colors. I like it particularly well with purple basil, purple peppers, red nasturtiums, and red flowering tobacco. What makes parsley even better is that it tastes good and is good for you!"
Aviva Levavi, Chicago Botanic Garden Fruit and Vegetable Island manager, Glencoe, Illinois

EDIBLE ANNUALS WITH ATTRACTIVE FLOWERS

Starry blue borage flowers floating in cold, creamy soup and lovely dill blossoms chopped and added to herbal butter make any meal special. Because they are delicate, edible flowers can seldom be purchased and are best grown in your own garden. German chamomile makes an interesting edging around taller plants like tomatoes or peppers. Dill, with its emphatic upright stems, looks great with low or mound-shaped plants like parsley or petunias. Pick the flowers while young and fresh. They fade quickly after opening.

Borage	blue flowers
Chamomile, German	white daisylike flowers
Dill	yellow flowers
Fennel	yellow flowers
Marigold, 'Lemon Gem'	small yellow flowers with citrus scent
Nasturtium	red, orange, or yellow flowers
Squash	yellow flowers

One bright edible flower found in almost every spring garden is the dandelion. Dr. Peter Gail has a passion for these prolific plants. He organizes a national Dandelion Cook-Off each year, held at Breitenbach Wine Cellars in Dover, Ohio, on the first Saturday in May. The best recipes from the Cook-Off have been compiled into the *Great Dandelion Cookbook: Recipes from the National Dandelion Cook-offs and Then Some* sold by Gail's Goosefoot Acres Center for Resourceful Living, PO Box 18016, Cleveland, OH 44118; 216–932–2145.

"In addition to being colorful and decorative, dandelions are one of the most nutritionally complete vegetables known to man. They contain twice as much of the healthful fatty acid lecithin as soybeans and also are rich in beta carotene, B vitamins, calcium, iron, and other nutrients. Dandelion flowers can be made into jelly and wine or dipped in batter and deep fried for a fritter that tastes like wild mushrooms. They also can be used in muffins, bread, pancakes, or waffles. Our favorite dandelion recipe is a dandy burger, a Grand Prize winner in the first Dandelion Cook-Off."

Peter A. Gail, Ph.D., Cleveland, Ohio-based ethnobotanist and author of The Dandelion Celebration: A Guide to Unexpected Cuisine

Ornamental Edibles in the Landscape

If you have enough room for a separate vegetable or herb garden, it will be the perfect place for pretty culinary plants. But culinary plants also can become hedges, screens, ground covers, and more. Here are some ideas to get your creative juices flowing.

ORNAMENTAL EDIBLES AS GROUND COVERS

Herbs, flowers, even vining vegetables can fill large swaths of space and serve as a unique ground cover. Here are two of the most reliable options for a moist, shady area.

Mint	creep aggressively on stolons
Sweet woodruff	fine foliage, creeping stems, white spring flowers

KATHLEEN GIPS'S FAVORITE FRAGRANT HERBS

Adding fragrance to a garden brings to life the sense of smell, which might otherwise be confined to the kitchen. Sometime the fragrance arrives gratis—released in the warm sun or when brushed by a passerby. But, in my experience, the most intense fragrance come when weeding. Uprooting over-abundant herbs creates a burst of fragrance, a reward for the gardener's diligence.

Kathleen Gips, who owns and operates the Village Herb Shop in Chagrin Falls, Ohio, understands well the pleasure of fragrance. She has made thousands of gallons of fragrant potpourri, blending dried herbs and flower petals to make into room-warming aromas. Here are some of her favorite fragrant herbs.

Lemon verbena	tender perennial with intensely lemon-scented leaves
Rose-scented geranium	divided leaves, pink flowers
Rose, 'Madamme Isaac Perierre'	large mauve flowers
Sweet woodruff	fine foliage, creeping stems, white spring flowers
Lemon thyme	low growing with lemon-scented leaves
Rosemary	tender perennial with needle-shaped leaves and blue flowers
Clove pinks	annuals with fragrant white or pink flowers
Bay	tender perennial with leathery fragrant leaves
Lavender	silver foliage, lavender flower spikes

"Sweet woodruff is a shade-loving ground cover that flourishes in the forests of Germany and in Midwestern gardens. This herb is easy to grow, providing a forest-green carpet around trees and shrubs in northern locations. The plant wears a carpet of dainty white flowers every May.

"Sweet woodruff is a traditional ingredient in May Wine. The leaves are infused with a sweet white wine for a day or two. Strain and add to equal amounts of strawberry juice and ginger ale then serve with strawberries and tiny sweet woodruff blossoms floating in a punch bowl.

"Sweet woodruff releases its scent after the leaves are dried. The mild vanilla scent is everlasting. Try a handful tied in a hanky in your dryer. This botanical is easily grown here providing many harvests for use in potpourri."

Kathleen Gips, author of Flora's Dictionary: The Victorian Language of Herbs and Flowers *and owner of the Village Herb Shop in Chagrin Falls, Ohio*

VINING EDIBLES FOR TRELLISES

Within a garden of vegetables, herbs, or low-growing flowers, you can create an eye-catching focal point by growing vegetable vines up on trellises. The Fruit and Vegetable Island at the Chicago Botanic Garden caught my interest the summer of 1996 with teepees made of bound poles covered with interwoven vines of squash, beans, and other aggressive climbers. Vining crops also can grow on trellises made of mesh held between two poles, chain-link fencing, chicken wire, or neat bean towers with string supports looped between a top and bottom wire hoop.

Beans, pole
Cucumbers
Malabar spinach
Peas
Squash, small fruited
Tomatoes

ESPECIALLY DECORATIVE CULTIVARS OF VEGETABLES

With some experience growing edible ornamentals, you will find that some cultivars are prettier than others. Currant and cherry tomatoes, for example, bear pretty cascading sprays of small fruit while most other tomatoes keep their fruit largely hidden beneath the foliage. Here are some of my favorite cultivars for color.

Amaranth 'Red Leaf Vegetable Amaranth'
Basil 'Purple Ruffles'
Beans 'Scarlet Runner'
Eggplant 'Rosa Bianca', 'Neon', 'Turkish'
Kohlrabi 'Purple Danube'
Strawberries
Lettuce 'Oak Leaf', 'Red Sails', 'Lolla Rossa', and other red leaf, frilly types
Mustard 'Red Giant'
Pepper 'Sweet Pickle', 'Pretty in Purple'
Strawberries 'Pink Panda', alpine
Swiss chard 'Rhubarb', 'Vulcan'
Tomato 'Red Currant', 'Sweet 100'

"Special herb groupings and interesting combinations can make a spectacular culinary garden. Bee balms of different shades grouped together make the quintessential July fireworks. Welsh onions have big, blowzy flowers and rim rod straight stems that lend a counter point in a tame herb bed. Against a backdrop of green, 'Thai' basil flowers take on a shimmering lavender haze when backlit by the sun."

ArLene Shannon, Greenfield Herb Garden, Shipshewana, Indiana

ESPECIALLY DECORATIVE CULTIVARS OF CULINARY HERBS FROM ARLENE SHANNON

Certain varieties of herbs are richer in color or have particularly interesting form or foliage and should be considered as edible ornamentals. 'African Blue' basil, for instance, has an enticing purple blush, and 'Berggarten' sage has a handsome round leaf and full shape. ArLene Shannon carefully examines the different nuances in the appearances of herbs at the Greenfield Herb Garden in Shipshewana, Indiana. There in the heart of Amish country, she propagates and displays over four hundred varieties of herbs. Here are some of her favorites.

BASIL CULTIVARS
'African Blue' basil
'Thai' basil

SAGE CULTIVARS
'Berggarten' Sage
'Tricolor' Sage
'Golden' Sage
'Purple' Sage
'Variegated Woodcote' Sage

OTHER HERBS
Welsh onion (*Allium fistulosum*)
Dwarf garden chives (*Allium schnittlauch*)
Angelica (*Angelica Archangelica*)
Bee Balm/Bergamot (*Monarda didyma*)
Sweet cicely (*Myrrhis odorata*)
Pennsylvania Dutch tea thyme (*Thymus pulegioides*)

CARLA NELSON'S TOP TEN HERBS FOR DECORATIVE PURPOSES

Carla Nelson, editor and publisher of *Herb Gatherings, The Newsletter for the Thymes* and author of *No Thyme to Cook Herbal Gourmet*, enjoys growing herbs that she can use indoors in dried arrangements and crafts. They include the following.

Basil: Dried seed pods can be made even more decorative if sprayed with gold spray paint.

Bee balm: Bright red feathery flowers used with white yarrow or coriander flowers and blue cornflowers make a perfect Fourth of July herbal centerpiece.

Butterfly weed (*Asclepias tuberosa*): Brilliant orange blossoms air-dry easily.

Chives: Blossoms cut before fully opened can be air dried upside down and used in culinary wreaths.

Elecampane: Flowers cut as they begin to go to seed can be air dried. Remove the fluffy seed casing for the exquisite burnished gold center and stiff golden rays emanating all around like a miniature glowing sun.

Lavender: Use easily dried flower spikes to make lavender wands, sachets, fragrant arrangements and on and on.

Marshmallow (*Althea officinalis*): Small pinkish-lavender flowers dried in silica gel are perfect for fairy wreaths.

Mountain mint, thin-leafed variety: This looks like a rosemary but is hardy in the Midwest and can stay green into December in a protected area. Cut it for fragrant holiday arrangements or dry it.

Tansy, especially 'Goldsticks': Sunny yellow clusters of button flowers work wonders in arrangements or wreaths, fresh or dried. Used them on an herbal Christmas tree for the effect of tiny lights.

Thyme: Dry leaf and flower sprigs in silica gel to use in small fairy wreaths.

GARDEN PLACEMENT

As a general rule, lower growing plants can be put toward the front of a garden as an edging, medium-height plants stand behind the front-runners, and tall plants, which may only reach their full height when mature or in bloom, bring up the rear. The following heights are only approximate and will vary depending on cultivar, season, and soil fertility.

LOW-GROWING ORNAMENTAL EDIBLES
Basil, bush
Lettuce
Parsley, curly
Thyme
Strawberries

MEDIUM-HEIGHT ORNAMENTAL EDIBLES
Basil, sweet
Cabbage
Chives
Eggplant
Fennel, Florence
Geraniums, scented
Kale
Lavender, compact cultivars
Parsley, Italian
Peppers, compact cultivars
Sage

TALLER ORNAMENTAL EDIBLES
Angelica, in bloom
Asparagus
Brussels sprouts, 'Rubine'
Dill
Jerusalem artichokes
Lovage, in bloom
Mint, pineapple
Peppers, taller cultivars
Sage, pineapple
Tomatoes, caged

ORNAMENTAL EDIBLES FOR HEDGES

If you don't mind putting a little more effort into maintenance, you can grow the following fruiting bushes or asparagus fronds as an informal or unclipped hedge. The berries have the advantages of white flowers and bright fruit, blueberry foliage turning scarlet in fall. Asparagus may produce red berries and golden fall foliage.

Asparagus
Blueberries
Raspberries, trellised
Blackberries, trellised

BULBS

It hardly seems like spring without crocus, daffodils, and other spring bulbs. Planted in the fall, they root unseen underground and burst forth when the time is right to inspire winter weary folks. True bulb lovers won't be in a hurry for summerlike temperatures but will enjoy a flowering season prolonged by cool spring weather.

There may be no finer artistry than a daffodil-covered hillside, like one on Cats Den Road near my old house in Chagrin Falls, Ohio. Also memorable are the oceans of daffodils arising through ivy at Cleveland Botanical Garden. Once forced for pots displayed at long-ago Botanical Garden spring shows, these daffodils were planted out in masses on this protected slope. Sadly, there was not a single bulb to be seen this spring at my new house in Indiana, but that problem will be corrected this fall.

Winter Aconite

Spring-flowering bulbs are not alone. For more fun with bulbs, you can grow summer flowering bulbs, most of which are not hardy in the Midwest. Their job is to provide riots of color in the summer. Treat them like annuals or store the bulbs (and similar underground structures such as tubers and corms) in a cool but frost-free place during winter.

Right Plant, Right Place

Bulbs, corms, and tubers use their swollen underground organs to store food, enough to power an incredible flower display. Daffodils, crocus, snowdrops, and squills can grow, flower, and multiply reliably in the Midwest if given moderately fertile, well-drained soil and allowed to gather sunshine until the foliage yellows. Tulips, nursery-grown under ideal conditions so

 Most spring bulbs do best in sun, which shines even under deciduous trees before the leaves emerge. But bulbs need their foliage to gather the sunshine and use it for photosynthesis. This means you should let the foliage remain loose and unhindered until it yellows.

the bulbs are strong, have an exceptional bloom when first planted. But Midwest conditions are not ideal for many tulips and future flower displays may be less satisfying. Match bulbs to growing conditions for many happy returns.

BULBS FOR SHADE

Some old trumpet daffodils planted on the north side of my former house sent out a few flowers and held their own reasonably well in the light shade. But when a new deck cut off their afternoon sun, they were through. If you have light shade, try some of the following bulbs that tolerate or prefer shade.

Wood
Anemone

Windflower (*Anemone blanda*)
European wood anemone (*Anemone nemorosa*)
Italian arum (*Arum italicum*)
Glory-of-the-snow (*Chionodoxa* spp.)
Crocus (*Crocus* spp.)
Winter aconite (*Eranthis* spp.)
Trout lily (*Erythronium* spp.)
Snowdrop (*Galanthus* spp.)
Netted iris (*Iris reticulata*)
Snowflake (*Leucojum* spp.)
Spanish bluebells (*Hyacinthus hispanica*)
Pushkinia (*Pushkinia scilloides*)
Scilla (*Scilla* spp.)

> If your yard is full of stiff clay, it's seldom enough to dig holes, amend them with sand, gravel, or peat, and plop bulbs down inside. Rain water will fill the holes up like bath tubs, regardless of what's inside. Since I've gardened in nothing but stiff clay for the last fifteen years, I've learned to put my bulbs in beds, large areas of amended soil that will let rain water flow through and out without encountering clay walls.

BULBS FOR MOIST SOILS

Fleshy underground bulbs can be highly prone to rotting if submerged in soggy soils, like an onion left in a sink full of water. Although they won't tolerate being submerged in a swamp, the following bulbs will grow nicely in moist, thick soils, like clay loams.

European wood anemone (*Anemone nemorosa*)
Winter aconite (*Eranthis hyemalis*)
Trout lily (*Erythronium* spp.)
Snowdrop (*Galanthus* spp.)
Snowflake (*Leucojum* spp.)
Daffodils (*Narcissus* spp.)

TULIPS MORE LIKELY TO PERENNIALIZE

Many tulips are treated like annuals in public gardens such as Fellows Riverside Park in Youngstown, Ohio, or Stan Hywet Hall in Akron, Ohio. Thousands are planted each fall and then dug up after flowering to replace with annuals. In your own garden, however, you may want tulips that have a chance of living for quite a while. The following are proven long-lived tulips.

> Darwin hybrids
> Foster tulip (*Tulipa Fosteriana*)
> Greig tulip (*Tulipa Greigii*)
> Waterlily tulip (*Tulipa Kaufmanniana*)
> Single early hybrids

Scott Kunst, always exploring for old-fashioned bulbs, occasionally stumbles on tulips decades old still growing and flowering in abandoned cemeteries or old vegetable gardens. Why have they remained thriving when other garden tulips may disappear after a few years? Kunst believes the difference is that neglected bulbs remain dry, not irrigated, in summer. For extending tulips lifetimes, consider some of Kunst's suggestions.

"Try this: Plant a few tulips where you never water and see how well they return. And avoid disturbing the soil by them when you garden. Beyond that, the basics include well-drained soil, full sun, regular fertilizing, and letting the foliage ripen. Some authorities also recommend deep planting—at least twelve inches deep.

"Then there's this traditional method; dig tulip bulbs up every summer, store in a cool dry spot, and replant in fall. You'll end up with more bulbs every year."

Scott Kunst, Old House Gardens, Ann Arbor, Michigan

BULBS LEAST LIKELY TO BE MUNCHED

If the much-awaited performance of newly planted bulbs never arrives, the bulbs have probably been eaten by pests. Deer love tulips. Squirrels and chipmunks adore crocus. Other burrowing rodents may make succulent bulbs into their winter snacks. One way to prevent these disappointing pest problems is to plant bulbs that are inedible or unappetizing. Or plant often-eaten bulbs in wire cages that will keep rodents out. Some seldom-snacked-on bulbs are listed below.

> Flowering onions (*Allium* spp.)
> Autumn crocus (*Colchicum* spp.)
> Crown imperial (*Fritillaria imperialis*)
> Naked lady (*Lycoris squamigera*)
> Daffodils (*Narcissus* spp.)
> Squills (*Scilla* spp.)

Narcissus

Bulbs through the Seasons

While bulbs are most famous for their spring bloom, they also can flower in late winter, summer, or fall. Crocus, a spring classic, also includes species that bloom in fall. One such autumn blooming crocus is *saffron* with lavender flowers containing tiny but flavorful grains of the spice saffron. Including hardy and tender bulbs in seasonal flowering sequences can provide pleasant rewards.

THE EARLIEST BULBS

The earliest flowers of spring, some of which might arrive during a mild spell in late winter, tend to be small and ground hugging. Although they look dainty, they are quite cold tolerant and usually perform well. For the best displays, plant them by the hundreds in large sweeps. that you can't miss. The only spring bloomer that occasionally disappoints is crocus, which close their flowers in cloudy weather and in some years may hardly open up at all.

> Windflower (*Anemone blanda*)
> Glory-of-the-snow (*Chionodoxa* spp.)
> Crocus (*Crocus* spp. and hyb.)
> Winter aconite (*Eranthis* spp.)
> Snowdrops (*Galanthus nivalis*)
> Siberian squill (*Scilla sibirica*)

DAFFODIL BLOOM SEQUENCE

I counted over two hundred daffodil cultivars with a diversity of different forms, shapes, colors, and bloom times in the 1997 Daffodil Mart catalogue. With this kind of big selection, it's easy to prolonging your daffodil enjoyment by planting early, midseason, and late bloomers. Here are some examples.

EARLY- BLOOMING DAFFODILS
'King Alfred'
'Ice Follies'
'Johann Strauss'
'Birma'

MIDSEASON- BLOOMING DAFFODILS
'Dutch Master'
'Lemon Glow'
'Mount Hood'
'Mon Cherie'

LATE- BLOOMING DAFFODILS
'Camelot'
'Caruso'
'Salome'
'Angel'
'Audubon'
'Merlin'

TULIP BLOOM SEQUENCE

Tulips tend to bloom after daffodils, the earliest tulips overlapping slightly with the later daffodils. Like daffodils, you can they are good to select for early, midseason, and late bloom.

EARLY- BLOOMING TULIPS

> *Single Early Tulips* such as 'Prince of Austria' and 'Apricot Beauty'
> *Double Early Tulips* such as 'Monte Carlo' and 'Peach Blossom'

MIDSEASON- BLOOMING TULIPS

> *Triumph Tulips* such as 'Garden Party' and 'Libretto'
> *Darwin Hybrids* such as 'Pink Impression" and 'Silverstream'
> *Single Late tulips* such as 'Dreamland' and 'Pink Jewel'

LATE- BLOOMING TULIPS

> *Tetraploid Single Late* such as 'Mrs. J.T. Scheepers' and 'Maureen'
> *Lily Flowering* such as 'Moonshine' and 'Queen of Sheba'
> *Double Late Tulips* such as 'Miranda' and 'Angelique'

An extended season of bloom is important at Stan Hywet Hall, the former estate of F.A. Seiberling, co-founder of the Goodyear Tire and Rubber Company in Akron, Ohio, now a historic house and garden open to the public.

"In our small, terrace-side gardens, we select an early- and late-season blooming bulb to plant every year. We often use early and late tulips, and occasionally use early hyacinths and late tulips, or daffodils and tulips for the extended color timeline. We use the same bulbs and color scheme in the terrace urns, which completes the display. We slip potted tulips into the urns in spring because the bulbs probably wouldn't survive the winter in the unprotected urns.

"We've also found it useful to match up the colors of early and late bloomers so that if there is a blast of spring heat and all the bulbs flower together, they'll still work well."

Carl Ruprecht, director of horticulture for Stan Hywet Hall, Akron, Ohio

HARDY BULBS FOR LATE SPRING OR SUMMER BLOOM

Some hardy, later blooming bulbs are natural companions for the perennial garden. They tend to have emphatic upright stems that contrast nicely with mound-shaped and creeping perennials. Here are a few examples.

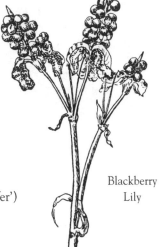

> Flowering onions (*Allium* spp.)
> Blackberry lily (*Belamcanda chinensis*)
> Lily (*Lilium* spp.)
> Magic lily (*Lycoris squamigera*)
> Lucifer crocosmia (*Crocosmia* × *crocosmiiflora* 'Lucifer')

Blackberry
Lily

HARDY BULBS FOR FALL BLOOM

Springlike bulbs flowering in autumn give some relief from all that gold and bronze foliage. The autumn crocuses are poisonous and have large, straplike leaves that appear in spring then die back in summer. They are best used amid ivy or periwinkle ground covers where the tall leaves won't intrude too much.

> Autumn crocus (*Colchicum* spp.)
> Fall flowering crocus (*Crocus sativus*, *C. speciosus*, and more)
> Madonna lily (*Lilium candidum*)
> Naked lady (*Lycoris squamigera*)

TENDER BULBS FOR SUMMER BLOOM

These bulbs (also tubers, corms, and more) come from tropical and semitropical warmer climes., bringing their tropical brilliance to Midwestern summer gardens. They blend nicely amid annual flowers and double as great cutting flowers. Gladiolus, stiffly upright and formal, can be planted beside a vegetable garden and used exclusively for cutting.

> Lily of the Nile (*Agapanthus africanus*)
> Tuberous begonia (*Begonia* hyb.)
> Elephant's ear (*Caladium* hyb.)
> Canna (*Canna* hyb.)
> Crinum lily (*Crinum* × *Powellii*)
> Montbretia (*Crocosmia* × *crocosmiiflora*)
> Dahlia (*Dahlia* hyb.)
> Pineapple lily (*Eucomis autumnalis*)
> Gladiolus (*Gladiolus* hyb.)
> Spider lily (*Hymenocallis narcissiflora*)
> Tuberose (*Polianthes tuberosa*)
> Tiger Flower (*Tigridia Pavonia*)
> Rain lily (*Zephyranthes* spp.)

"In 1997, we made an entire bed of summer bulbs but found that they needed other plants such as annuals to compliment them. The reason is that a lot of summer bulbs, including tigridia, ilxia, Crocosmia, crinum, and freesia, bloom quite spectacularly, but only for a short time. In contrast, cannas, elephant ears, and tuberous begonias will bloom most of the summer. Purple-flowered globe amaranth, scarlet zinnias, "Purple Wave" petunias, and "Purple Ruffles" basil fill in nicely around all of them."
David Bird, horticulturist at Powell Gardens in Kingsville, Missouri

Bulbs in the Landscape

Hardy bulbs have a habit of coming and going, the foliage often dying back by summer and leaving little clue to where the bulbs are lying dormant. Put spring flowering bulbs where they won't be forgotten and mistakenly dug up. They can be naturalized below deciduous trees and shrubs or at the edge of the lawn. Or plant them around perennials like hardy geraniums, daylilies, hostas, baptesia, peonies, and Siberian iris. Other great landscape ideas are as near as your local botanical garden or public park.

KEITH KAISER ON BULB COMBINATIONS FOR SIMULTANEOUS BLOOM

When I visited Fellows Riverside Gardens in Youngstown, Ohio, in late April, I was delighted by the beautiful combinations of bulbs and other plants flowering simultaneously. The garden has about 40,000 bulbs in bloom every year, with 25,000 new bulbs planted each fall. Keith Kaiser, assistant horticulture director for Fellows Riverside Gardens and Mill Creek MetroParks, shared some of the most outstanding companion plantings he's devised there.

Single Early tulip 'Apricot Beauty' and Triandrus narcissus 'Thalia'

Triumph tulip 'Attila' and Single Late tulip 'Pink Supreme'

Double narcissus 'Sir Winston Churchill' and Single Late tulip 'Kingsblood'

Miniature narcissus 'Tete-a-Tete' and blue windflower (*Anemone blanda* 'Blue')

Japanese kerria (*Kerria japonica* 'Pleniflora'), Korean spice viburnum (*Viburnum Carlesii*), and redbud (*Cercis canadensis*) overlapping with mid- to late -season tulips

Single Late tulip 'Duke of Wellington', Single Late tulip 'Temple of Beauty', and Single Late tulip 'Queen of the Night'

Johnny Jump-Up

Double Early tulip 'Carlton' and Double Early tulip 'Peach Blossom'

Leopard's bane (*Doronicum cordatum*), with grape hyacinth (*Muscari* 'Blue Spike'), 'White Splendor' windflower (*Anemone blanda* 'White Splendor'), and Johnny jump-up (*Viola tricolor*)

"Design your bulb displays by using them en mass to fill a large area. Or put them in little groupings, using odd numbers of each bulb type and repeating the groupings throughout the garden or bed. Look at other gardens to see what is in bloom at the same time. Then, as long as the flower colors harmonize well, plant them in your garden for beautiful displays."
Keith Kaiser, assistant horticulture director, Mill Creek MetroParks and Fellows Riverside Gardens, Youngstown, Ohio

CHARLES GLEAVES'S FAVORITE BULBS
FOR NATURALIZING

The Indianapolis Museum of Art, surrounded by fifty-two acres of cultivated grounds, has sunny formal gardens and naturalized woodland gardens. In spring, the naturalized areas glow with large sweeps of durable bulbs such as the followingese recommended by horticulturist Charles Gleaves.

Flowering onion (*Allium aflatunense*)
European wood anemone (*Anemone nemorosa*)
Winter aconite (*Eranthis hyemalis*)
Spanish bluebells (*Hyacinthoides hispanica*)
Naked lady (*Lycoris squamigera*)
Baby Boom daffodil (*Narcissus* 'Baby Boom')
February Gold daffodil (*Narcissus* 'February Gold')
Pipit daffodil (*Narcissus* 'Pipit')
Poet's daffodil (*Narcissus poeticus*)

BULBS WITH HANDSOME FOLIAGE

Flowers aren't everything when it comes to bulbs. The following bulbsBulbs such as the following are as famous for their foliage as for their blossoms. The caladiums, with brightly colored, spreading leaves, are particularly spectacular. BecauseSince they are tender, treat them as annuals or store indoors during winter.

Caladium (*Caladium* hyb.)
Hardy cyclamen (*Cyclamen* spp.)
Gregii tulips (*Tulipa Greigii*)

SCOTT KUNST'S FAVORITE OLD-FASHIONED BULBS
FOR THE MIDWEST

By growing old- fashioned plants, just like those you might remember from your grand-mother's garden, your yard takes on a new dimension. It connects you with the past and the many gardeners who have gone before you. Scott Kunst, an avid collector of old- fashioned bulbs from Ann Arbor, Michigan, found that many were being dropped out of modern catalogues. So he started his own catalogue of historical classics.

In a lot of ways, these bulbs are similar to modern bulbs but most have a special virtue that has kept them around for decades or even centuries. Some may be tough and need less coddling. Others arecan be more fragrant. Because they are closer to their wild predecessors, some may be smaller and more graceful, not beefed up like many newer hybrids. Here are some of Kunst's old -time favorites.

CROCUS
Crocus (They prefer the slightly alkaline soil so are prevalent through much of the Midwest.)

'Cloth of Gold' (1587; the only snow crocus common in American gardens before 1930)

'Paulis Potter' (1920; rich, red purple color)

HYACINTHS

(These are best in Zone 5 and warmer areas.)

'Bismark' (1875; has returned dependably in Kunst's garden and has a rich purple flower)

'Distinction' (1880; unique, small, beet-root maroon flowers)

'Gipsy Queen' (1927; soft, apricot-colored flowers)

TULIPS

(Like crocus, these do best in slightly alkaline soil.)

'Greuze' (1891; late blooming, dark purple, tall and willowy, often with a cluster of blooms from one bulb)

'Prince of Austria' (1860; sweetly fragrant, red flowers maturing almost to orange)

Tulip Schrenkii(1585; early-blooming dwarf with red-edged yellow flowers)

DAFFODILS

'Barrii Conspicuus' (1869; dainty flower with short, orange-rimmed cup and pale yellow petals)

Lent lily (*Narcissus Pseudonarcissus*; 1570; long yellow trumpets and slightly forward twisted petals for informal look)

'W. P. Milner' (1869; miniature with nodding trumpets of pale yellow)

SNOWDROPS

Single snowdrop (*Galanthus nivalis*; 1597; the earliest bloom of spring, short white bells, spreads happily in light shade)

MAIL-ORDER PLANT SOURCES

Although you'll generally get larger plants at garden centers, sometimes local growers simply don't grow a special plant that you want. You can turn to mail-order catalogs to find almost any plant under the sun. A few of these companies charge a small fee for their catalogs, which abound with useful information.

Arrowhead Alpines
PO Box 857
Fowlerville, MI 48836

Bluestone Perennials
7211 Middle Ridge Road
Madison, WI 44057-3096
800-852-5243

Atlee Burpee Co.
Warminster, PA 18974
800-888-1447

Companion Plants
7247 N. Coolville Ridge
Road
Athens, OH 45701
614-592-4643

The Cook's Garden
PO Box 535
Londonberry, VT 05148
800-457-9703

The Daffodil Mart
7463 Heath Trail
Gloucester, VA 23061
800-ALL-BULB

Garden City Seeds
778 Highway 93 North
Hamilton, MT 59840
406-961-4877

Garden Place
(field-grown perennials)
6780 Heisley Road
PO Box 388
Mentor, OH 44061-0388
216-255-3705

Girard Nurseries
PO Box 428
Geneva, OH 44041
216-466-2881

Historical Roses
1657 W. Jackson Street
Painesville, OH 44077
216-357-7270

Johnny's Select Seed
Foss Hill Road
Albion, ME 04910-9731
207-437-4301

Klehm's Nursery
4210 N. Duncan Road
Champaign, IL 61821
800-553-3715

Logee's Greenhouses
141 North Street
Danielson, CT 06239-1939
860-774-8038

Milaeger's Gardens
4838 Douglas Avenue
Racine, WI 53402-2498
800-669-9956

Nichols Garden Nursery
1190 N. Pacific Highway
Albany, OR 97321-4580
541-967-8406

Old House Gardens
(historic bulbs)
536 Third Street
Ann Arbor, MI 48103
313–995–1486

Park Seed
1 Parkton Avenue
Greenwood, SC 29647-
0001
864-223-7333

Prairie Nursery
(prairie plants)
PO Box 306
Westfield, WI 53964
608-296-2741

The Roseraie at Bayfields
(roses)
PO Box R
Waldboro, ME 04572-0919
207-832-6330

Seed Saver's Exchange
3076 N. Winn Road
Decorah, IA 52101
319-382-5990

Shady Hill Gardens
(geraniums)
821 Walnut Street
Batavia, IL 60510-2999
708-879-5665

Shady Oaks Nursery
(perennials for shade)
112 10th Avenue SE
Waseca, MN 56093
800-504-8006

Southmeadow Fruit Gardens
Box SM
Lakeside, MI 49116
616-469-2865

Sunnybrook Farms
(herbs and perennials)
PO Box 6
Chesterland, OH 44026
216-729-7232

Thompson and Morgan
PO Box 1308
Jackson, NJ 08527-0308

Wayside Gardens
Hodges, SC 29695-0001
800-845-1124

White Flower Farm
PO Box 50
Litchfield, CT 06759-0050
800-503-9624

INDEX